This book is for all the new baby boys and baby girls

May your lights shine magnificently and brightly…

Asher Abraham

First Published 2006
Lulu™ Publishing
ISBN 97 81 41161618 9

A-Z of Hebrew Bibilical Names, Meanings, Bible References, Geneology and Pronunciations

This page is for you to list your Top 20 Baby Names

Baby Names that are listed as being *Male* can be used as *Female* names also

(There is a place to take Notes at the back of this book)

1.
2.
3.
4.
5.
6.
7.
8.
9.
10.
11.
12.
13.
14.
15.
16.
17.
18.
19.
20.

A-Z Of Hebrew Bibilical Names, Meanings, Bible References, Geneology and Pronunciations

A

AARON The son of Amram and Jochebad and the brother of Moses and Miriam **(Numbers 26:59)**. Aaron was the first High Priest of the Hebrews ***Meaning*** Mountain of Strength or The Illuminator (Aa-ron) Male

ABDI A Levite grandfather of Ethan. **(1 Chron 6:44)** ***Meaning*** My Servant (Ab-di) Male

ABEDNEGO Babylonian name of Azariah one of Daniels three prophets **(Daniel 1:7)** ***Meaning*** Servant of Nego and Protector (A-bed-nego) Male

ABELThe second son of Eve and Adam. Abel was a keeper of sheep, Abel was put to death by his brother Cain **(Genesis 4:2)** ***Meaning*** Emptiness, Vanity (A-bell) Male

ABIAH A wife of Hezron and mother of Ashur **(I Chronicles 2:24)** ***Meaning*** My Father is Lord (A-bi-a) Female

ABIATHAR A Priest, the son of Ahimelech from Elis family **(1 Kings 2:27)** ***Meaning*** Father of Abundance (A-bia-thar) Male

ABIEL The father of Kish and Grandfather of King Saul. See KISH for details **(1 Samuel 9:1)** ***Meaning*** Father or Possessor (Ab-i-el) Male

ABIDA A son of Midian, and grandson of Abraham by Ketura **(Genesis 25:4) (I Chronicles 1:33)**. ***Meaning*** Father of Knowledge (A-bi-da) Male

ABIDAN The head of the tribe of Benjamin at the Exodus **(Numbers 1:11, 2:22)** ***Meaning*** Father of Judgment (A-bi-dan) Male

ABIEZER A son of Hammeloketh (His mother). A decendant of Manasseh from the tibe of Manasseh **(I Chronicles 7:18)** ***Meaning*** Father of Help (Ab-i-ee-zer) Male

ABIGAIL The daughter of Nahash first married to Nabal, then to David, she was the mother of Davids second son Chileab **(I Samuel 25:2-42, II Samuel 3:3)**. Another was Abigail who Married Jether and was the mother of Amasa, she was the daughter of Jesse and great granddaughter of Boaz and Ruth **(Ruth 4:17)** her brothers were Eliab, Abinadab, Shimea, Nethanel, Raddai, Ozem, King David and her sister was Zeruiah. ***Meaning*** Leader of Joy or Leader of the Dance (Ab-i-gail) Female

ABIHAIL A wife of King Rehoboam **(II Chronicles 11:18-19)** Another was the father of Esther **(Esther 2:15, 9:29)**. ***Meaning*** Father of Might (Abi-hail) Male/Female

ABIHU A son of Aaron by Elisheba **(Exodus 6:23)** he accompanied Moses and Aaron on Mount Sinai **(Exodus 24:1)** ***Meaning*** Worshipper of God (A-bi-hu) Male

ABIJAH or ABIAH King of Judah, son of King Rehoboam his mother was Maachah. Another was the daughter of Absalom **(II Chronicles 11:17-22, I Kings 15:1,2)**. Another was the second son of Samuel **(1 Sam 8:1,2)** ***Meaning*** Worshipper of the Lord or My father is the Lord (Abi- ah) Male/Female

A-Z Of Hebrew Bibilical Names, Meanings, Bible References, Geneology and Pronunciations

ABIMAEL One of the thirteen sons of Joktan his brothers were Almodad, Sheleph, Hazarmaveth, Jerah, Hadoram, Uzal, Diklah, Ebal, Sheba, Ophir, Havilah and Jobab. **(Genesis 10:25-30)** ***Meaning*** My Father is Truly God (A-bim-a-il) Male

ABIMELECH A Canaanite King of Gerar. Also the son of Gideon to a concubine **(Judges 8:30-31)**. Abimelech later killed all but one of his seventy half-brothers in order to become King of Shechem **(Judges 9:6)** ***Meaning*** My Father is the King (A-bim-el-leck) Male

ABINOAM A son of King Saul **(1 Sam 31:2)** ***Meaning*** Father of Kindness (A-bin-o-am) Male

ABIRAM The son of Eliab from the tribe of Reuben. His brother was Dathan **(Numbers 16)** ***Meaning*** Father of Height (A-by-ram) Male

ABISHAI First born son of Zeruiah sister of David. Abishai was the brother of Joab and Asahel **(1 Chron 2:16)** ***Meaning*** A Desired Gift (A-bi-shy) Male

ABISHUA The grandson of Benjamin **(1 Chr. 8:4).** ***Meaning*** Father of Wealth and Very Fortunate. (A-bi-shew-a) Male

ABITAL A wife of King David and the mother of Davids fifth son, Shephatiah **(2 Sam 3:4)** ***Meaning*** Father of Dew (A-by-tal) Female

ABIUD Son of Zerubbabel ancestor of Jesus **(Matthew 1:13)** ***Meaning*** Father of Praise (A-by-ud) Male

ABNER Son of Ner and cousin of King Saul, he was the head of Sauls army **(1Sam 14:50,51)** ***Meaning*** Father of Light (Ab-ner) Male

ABRAHAM also ABRAM A son of Terah and father of Ishmael, Isaac and many others, he was first called Abram **(Genesis 11:27)**. His first wife was Sarah (Sarai) who was his half-sister (they had the same father, but different mothers) **(Genesis 20:1, 12)** ***Meaning*** Father of a Multitude (Ab-ra-ham) Male

ABRAM see ABRAHAM ***Meaning*** High Exalted Father (Ab-ram) Male

ABSOLOM A son of King David by Maacah **(2 Samuel 3:3, 1 Kings 1:6)** ***Meaning*** Father of Peace (Ab-sol-lom) Male

ACHAN A son of Carmi from the tribe of Judah **(Joshua 7)** ***Meaning*** One who Troubles or One who Trys (Ay-Kan) Male

ACHIOR Leader of the Ammonites **(Judith 5:5)** ***Meaning*** From Trouble to Hope (Ay-ki-or) Male

ACHISH A Philistine King of Gath who helped David **(1Samuel 27)** ***Meaning*** And Thus it is (Ay-kish) Male

ACHSAH Calebs daughter and wife of Othniel **(Judges 1:12)** ***Meaning*** Anklet (Ak-sa) Female

A-Z Of Hebrew Bibilical Names, Meanings, Bible References, Geneology and Pronunciations

ADAH A wife of Lamech (Lamech was the son of Methusael) and a descendant of Cain **(Genesis 4:18-19)**. Another was the daughter of Elon the Hittite, she was a wife of Esau and the mother of Eliphaz **(Genesis 36:2, 4)** ***Meaning*** Ornament (Ae-da)

ADAIAH Father of Jedidah and grandfather of Josiah **(II Kings 22:1)** ***Meaning*** Witness of God (Aa-day-yah) Male

ADALIA A son of Haman **(Esther 9:8)** ***Meaning*** Refuge of God or Just Noble One (Aa-day-lia) Male

ADAM First man of the Bible **(Genesis 1:26-27, 2: 5:1-2)** Adam is also a city on the east bank of Jordan ***Meaning*** Ruddy or Red (Aa-dam) Male

ADBEEL The third of the twelve sons of Ishmael and brother of Nebaioth, Kedar, Mibsam, Mishma, Dumah, Massa, Hadad, Tema, Jetur, Naphish and Kedemah **(Genesis 25) (I Chronicles 1:29)** ***Meaning*** A Miracle of God (Ad-be-el) Male

ADDON From the book of Nehemiah **(Nehemiah. 7:61)** ***Meaning*** Low (Aa-don) Male

ADIEL The father of Azmaveth, who was treasurer under King David and Solomon **(1 Chr. 27:25)** Another was the head of the tribe of Simeon **(1 Chr. 4:36)** Another was a Priest **(1 Chr. 9:12)** ***Meaning*** Ornament of God (Aa-dee-el) Male

ADINA One of Davids warriors **(1 Chr. 11:42)** who was a Reubenite ***Meaning*** Slender (A-dee-na) Male

ADONAI Another name for the Lord God ***Meaning*** God or Lord of All (A-don-eye) Male/Female

ADONIKAM He had six hundred threescore and seven children (667). Three of these were Eliphelet, Jeiel and Shemaiah **(Ezra 8:13)** ***Meaning*** The Lord is Raised (A-don-nye-kam) Male

ADONIJAH A son of King David by Haggith **(2 Samuel 3:4)** ***Meaning*** My Lord is Jehovah (A-don-nee-ja) Male

ADONIRAM An official of King Davids and of Solomon **(2 Samuel 20:24)** ***Meaning*** Unity (A-don-nee-ram) Male

ADRIEL The husband of Merab (Merab was King Sauls daughter) **(1 Samuel 18:17)** ***Meaning*** Flock of God (Ae-dree-el) Male

AHAB A King of Israel, son of King Omri **(I Chronicles 16: 28-30)** he had seventy sons **(II Kings 7:1)** including two Kings of Israel, Ahaziah and Jehoram **(I Kings 22:40, 51) (II Kings 3:1)** and a daughter who married another King of Judah. Jezebel was Ahabs wife **(I Kings 16: 30-31)** ***Meaning*** My Fathers Brother (Ae-hab) Male

AHASUERUS King of Persia whose history is covered in Esther **(Esther 1)** Another was the Father of Darius **(Daniel 9:1)** ***Meaning*** A Prince and Chief Male (Ae-ha-zoo-ear-rus) Male

AHAZ One of the many Kings of Judah **(2 Kings 16:1)** ***Meaning*** Possessor (Ae-haz) Male

A-Z Of Hebrew Bibilical Names, Meanings, Bible References, Geneology and Pronunciations

AHAZIAH One of the Kings of Israel, the son of King Ahab **(I Kings 22:40)** he died without having any sons and was succeeded as King of Israel by Jehoram **(II Kings 1:17-18)** ***Meaning*** Held by the Lord (Ae-a-zye-ah) Male

AHIJA, AHIJAH, AHIAH Father of Baasha. Baasha became King of Israel. **(I Kings 15:27-29)** Ahija was of the house of Issachar **(I Kings 15:27)** (The fifth son of Jacob and the founder of one of the twelve tribes). There are many men called Ahijah in the bible. ***Meaning*** Brother of Jehovah (Aa-hye-ja) (Aa-hye-ya) Male

AHIAM One of Davids heroes **(2 Sam. 23:33, 1 Chr. 11:35)** ***Meaning*** My Mothers Brother or Uncle (Aa-hye-am) Male

AHIKAM He rescued Jeremiah from certain death **(Jeremiah 26:24)** Another was the son of Shaphan and the father of another Ahikam and grandfather of Gedaliah (**2 Kings 22:12)** ***Meaning*** Brother of Support. (Aa-hye-kam) Male

AHIMAAZ The son of Zadok and the father of Azariah **(I Chronicles 6:8-9)** ***Meaning*** Brother of Anger (Aa-hye-ma-az) Male

AHIMAN A legendary giant among the Anakim of Hebron **(Numbers 13:22) (Joshua 15:14) (Judges 1:10)** ***Meaning*** A Gift or Brother of a Gift (Aa-hye-man) Male

AHIMELECH The son of Ahitub and father of Abiathar **(1 Sam. 22:20-23)** A descendant of Eli. ***Meaning*** Brother of the King (Aa-him-a-lek) Male

AHINOAM A wife of David **(I Samuel 25:43)** and the mother of Davids firstborn son, Amnon **(II Samuel 3:2)** ***Meaning*** Of Pleasantness (Aa-hin-o-am) Female

AHIO One of the sons of Beriah **(1 Chr. 8:14)** There are three men named Ahio in the bible not much is known of them ***Meaning*** Brotherly (Aa-hye-o) (A-hi-o) Male

AHITHOPHEL Counsellor to David **(II Samuel 15:12)** and father of Eliam **(II Samuel 23:34)** ***Meaning*** Bored (Aa-hith-o-fell) Male

AHITUB In the Levitical line of Eleazer, he was the son of Amariah and the father of Zadok **(I Chronicles 6:7-8)** Also the father of Ahimelech ***Meaning*** Of Goodness (Aa-hye-tub) Male

AHLAI The daughter of Sheshan, she was given to Sheshans Egyptian servant **(I Chronicles 2:31)** ***Meaning*** Beseeching and Expectant (Aa-Lye-ee) Female

AHOLIBAMA A wife of Esau and descendant of Zibeon the Hivite **(Genesis 36:2)**.***Meaning*** My Tabernacle is Exalted or Exalted One (Aa-ho-lee-barm-a) Female

AHIJAH The father of Baasha, one of the Kings of Israel **(I Kings 15:33)** ***Meaning*** Jehovah is My Brother (Aa-hye-ah) Male

AIAH The father of Rizpah, Sauls concubine **(2 Samuel 3:7)** ***Meaning*** Raven (Ae-ya) Male

A-Z Of Hebrew Bibilical Names, Meanings, Bible References, Geneology and Pronunciations

AKILIA or AZURA/KALI AZURA or AKELMIA The Second daughter of Adam and Eve, she married Seth her brother (not mentioned in the KJV) **(Genesis 39:12)** ***Meaning*** Keen (A-kee-lee-a) Female

ALEXANDER A relative of Annas the High Priest present when Peter and John were examined before the Sanhedrim **(Acts 4:6)** There are lots of Alexanders in the bible ***Meaning*** Defender of Man (A-lex-an-der) Male

ALMODAD One of the thirteen sons of Joktan, his brothers were Sheleph, Hazarmaveth, Jerah, Hadoram, Uzal, Diklah, Ebal, Abimael, Sheba, Ophir, Havilah and Jobab **(Genesis 10:25-30)** ***Meaning*** The Measure of God (Al-mo-dad) Male

AMARIAH In the Levitical line of Eleazer, he was the son of Azariah and the father of Ahitub **(I Chronicles 6:11)** ***Meaning*** Said by God (Am-a-riah) Male

AMASA The son of Abigail (Abigail was a sister of King David) **(1 Chr. 2:17) (2 Samuel 17:25)** ***Meaning*** Of a Burden (A-may-sa) Male

AMAZIAH A King of Judah. Also a Levite son of Hilkiah of the descendants of Ethan **(1 Chr. 6:45).** There are at least four Amaziahs in the bible ***Meaning*** Strengthened by Jehovah (Am-a-zye-ah) Male

AMELEK Son of Eliphaz and Timna and grandson of Esau **(Genesis 36:2)** he was the founder of the Amelekites ***Meaning*** Dweller in the valley (A-mel-lek) Male

AMITTAI The father of Jonah from the tribe of Zebulun **(2 Kings 14:25)** ***Meaning*** One who is True (A-mit-tye) Male

AMMIHUD He was one of the Chiefs of the Naphtali tribe and father of Pedahel **(Numbers 34:28)** Another was the Son of Laadan **(1Ch 7:26)** and also father of Elishama **(Numbers 1:10; 2:18)** Also the father of Shemuel **(Numbers 34:20)**. Another was the father of Talmai, King of Geshur who Absalom fled from after the murder of Amnon **(2Samuel 13:37)** ***Meaning*** People of Glory or Man of Glory (Am-mee-hud) Male

AMNON The first born son of King David, he was born to Davids wife Ahinoam **(2 Samuel 13)** ***Meaning*** Faithful One (Am-non) Male

AMON A King of Judah. The prophet Micaiah was in his custody **(1 Kings 22:26, 2 Chr. 18:25)** ***Meaning*** The Builder (Ay-mon) Male

AMOS One of the Twelve Prophets **(Amos 1:1, 7:14, 15)** ***Meaning*** Born (Ay-mos) Male

AMRAM A decendant of Levi, Kohath was his father. The husband of Jochebed (Jochebed was his auntie) and the father of Moses, Aaron and Miriam **(Exodus 2:1 6:20) (Numbers 26:59)** ***Meaning*** Kindred of the High and Exalted (Am-ram) Male

AMRAPHEL also HAMMURABI The sixth King of Babylon **(Genesis 14)** ***Meaning*** Speaker of Secrets or Speaker of Sacred Secrets (Am-ra-fell) Male

A-Z Of Hebrew Bibilical Names, Meanings, Bible References, Geneology and Pronunciations

ANAH A son of Seir the Duke of Edom, an ancestor of Aholibamah, his siblings were Shobal, Zibeon, Anah, Dishon, Ezer, Dishan and his sister was Timna **(Genesis 36:20)** ***Meaning*** Speech (A-na) Male

ANAKIM The descendants of Anak who occupied Palestine before the arrival of the Israelites. **(Joshua 11:21) (Numbers 13:33) (Deut. 9:2)** ***Meaning*** The Watcher (An-na-kim) Male/Female

ANAMIM His father was Mizraim (of the early tribe Mizraim). His brothers were Ludim, Lehabim, Caphtorim, Naphtuhim, Pathrusim and Casluhim (from whose line came the Philistines) **(Genesis 10:13)** ***Meaning*** A Fountain (An-na-mim) Male/Female

ANANIAS or ANNAEUS or ANNAS A common Jewish name, the Greek form of Hananiah **(Tobit 5:13)** There are four Ananias in the bible one was a High Priest. Another was the husband of Sapphira **(Acts 4,5; 9,11)** ***Meaning*** God is Gracious (Ana-nye-ess) Male

ANDREW He was one of Jesus Disciples and the brother of Simon Peter. Andrew was the disciple of John the Baptist before he became Jesus Disciple **(Matthew 4:18,10:2) (John 1:44)** ***Meaning*** A Strong Man (An-drew) Male

APOLLONIA A city of Macedonia which Paul and Silas pass through **(Acts 17:1)** The feminine form of the Greek God Apollo ***Meaning*** God of Truth and Light (Ap-pol-low-nia) Female

APOLLOS A Jewish man from Alexandria who was very well versed in the scriptures **(Acts 18:24)** name taken from the Greek God Apollo ***Meaning*** God of Truth and Light (Ap-pol-loss) Male

APPHIA A female Christian at Colosse could have been Philemons wife as her name was in Pauls letter to Philemon **(Philemon 1:2)** ***Meaning*** Increasing (A-fee-a) Female

APPAIM Son of Nadab and father of Ishi **(I Chronicles 2:30-31)** ***Meaning*** Face or Nostrils (Aa-pay-im) Male

ARAM One of the five sons of Shem he was Noahs grandson. His brothers were Elam, Asshur, Arphaxahad and Lud **(Genesis 10:1,22)** he was the father of Uz, Hul, Gether and Mash **(Genesis 10:23)** ***Meaning*** High (A-ram) Male

ARAN A descendant of Seir **(Genesis 36:28)** ***Meaning*** Wild Goat (A-ran) Male

ARCHELAUS The son of Herod the first **(Matthew 2:22)** ***Meaning*** Ruler of The People (Ar-ka-lay-us) Male

ARCHIPUSS One of the people the letter to Philemon was sent to **(Philemon 2)** ***Meaning*** Master of Horses (Ar-kip-us)

ARDON The last of the three sons of Caleb by his first wife Azubah his brothers were Jesher and Shobab **(1 Chr. 2:18, 19)** ***Meaning*** Bronze (Ar-don) Male

ARELI One of the sons of Gad **(Genesis 46:16)** ***Meaning*** Lion of God (Ar-re-lye) Male

A-Z Of Hebrew Bibilical Names, Meanings, Bible References, Geneology and Pronunciations

ARETAS The name of a few Nabatean Kings **(2 Mac 4:7)** ***Meaning*** Agreeable (Ar-re-tus) Male

ARIDATHA A son of Haman **(Esther 9:8)** ***Meaning*** Flowering Field (Ari-day-tha) Male/Female

ARIMATHEA The city of Josephs birth **(Matthew 27:57)** ***Meaning*** Lion Dead to The Lord (Ari-may-thea) Male

ARISTOBULUS A Jew and local of Alexandria and teacher of King Ptolemy VI Philometer and of a Priestly family, his son was Alexander-Janneus **(2 Mac 1:10 2:18)** ***Meaning*** A Good Counselor (Aris-toe-bew-lus) Male

ARIUS The King of Sparta from the line of Abraham. **(1 Mac 12:7)** ***Meaning*** of the Lion or Eagle (Ari-us) Male

ARMONI A son of Rizpah, Sauls concubine **(2 Samuel 21:8)** ***Meaning*** One from the Palace or Castle or One From a High Place (Ar-mo-nee) Male

ARPHAXAHAD He was one of the five sons of Shem and Noahs grandson. His brothers were Elam, Asshur, Lud and Aram **(Genesis 10:1,22)** he was the father of Salah **(Genesis 10:24)** ***Meaning*** The Healer (Ar-fak-sad) Male

ARVAD A Phoenician city **(Ezekiel 27:8)** ***Meaning*** The Wanderer or The Voyager (Ar-vad) Male

ARTEMIS A Greek Goddess corresponding to Diana **(Acts 19)** ***Meaning*** Mother or Goddess (Ar-tee-miss) Female

ASA A King of Judah and son of Abijah. He was greatly honored by his people. He was the father of Jehoshaphet **(I Kings 15:9-13, II Chronicles 15:16)** ***Meaning*** Physician or Healer (Ae-sa) Male

ASAHEL He was the youngest son of Zeruiah, Davids Nephew. His brothers were Joab and Abishai **(2 Samuel 2:18, 19)** ***Meaning*** Made by God (A-sar-hill) Male

ASAIAH A servant of King Josiah **(2 Kings 22:12,14)** ***Meaning*** The Lord Has Bought About (A-zay-yah) Male

ASENATH Daughter of Potiphera an Egyptian Priest and wife of Joseph given to him by Pharaoh **(Genesis 41:45)** ***Meaning*** Gift ofThe Sun God (As-ee-nath) Female

ASHAN A Levite town of Judah **(Joshua 21:16)** ***Meaning*** Smoke (Ae-shan) Male/Female

ASHER The eighth of Jacobs twelve sons. He was the founder of the Tribe of ISRAEL, ASHER. He was the second son of Zilpah (The handmaid of Jacobs wife Leah) **(Genesis 30:12-13)**. His brothers were Benjamin, Dan, Gad, Issachar, Joseph, Judah, Levi, Naphtali, Reuben, Simeon and Zebulun. His sister was Dinah ***Meaning*** Happy and Fortunate (A-sha) Male

ASHIMA The name of a God of the people of Hamath ***Meaning*** Limitless One (A-shy-ma) Male/Female

A-Z Of Hebrew Bibilical Names, Meanings, Bible References, Geneology and Pronunciations

ASHKELON One of the cities forming Pentapolis **(Joshua 13:3)** ***Meaning*** A Small Root (Ash-kee-lon) Female/Male

ASHKENAZ One of the three sons of Gomer **(Genesis 10:3)** ***Meaning*** A Fire That Spreads (Ash-ka-naz) Male

ASHUR A son of Abiah and Hezron who was born after his fathers death according to the KJV translation **(I Chronicles 2:24)** Some bibles say that Caleb married Ephrathah (His fathers widow) and they had a son named Ashur ***Meaning*** Beautiful Black Dark (A-sure) Male

ASHVATH One of the sons of Japhlet from the tribe of Asher, his brothers were Pasach and Bimhal **(1 Ch 7:33)** ***Meaning*** Worked Strong Like Iron (Ah-vath) (Male)

ASPATHA A Son of Haman his brothers were Parshandatha and Dalphon **(Esther 9:7)** ***Meaning*** Self Sufficient (Ass-par-tha) Male

ASSHUR One of the five sons of Shem he was Noahs grandson. His brothers were Elam, Arphaxahad, Lud and Aram **(Genesis 10:1,22)** ***Meaning*** Beautiful Black Dark (A-sure) Male

ASSIR A son of King Jehoiachin of Judah **(I Chronicles 3:17)** ***Meaning*** Fettered or Restrained (A-sir) Male

ATARAH The mother of Onam a wife of Jerahmeel **(I Chronicles 2:9, 2:25-27)** ***Meaning*** A Crown (At-tar-ra) Female

ATHALIA A daughter of King Ahab of Israel, a wife of King Jehoram (Joram) of Judah. The mother of King Ahaziah of Judah **(II Chronicles 22:2)** A ruler of Judah **(II Kings 11:3)** ***Meaning*** For Whom God Afflicts (Ath-ar-lee-a) Female

ATTALIA A port city of Asia Minor **(Acts 14:25)** ***Meaning*** One Who Increases or Who Sends (At-a-lee-a) Male/Female

ATTAI He was the grandson of Sheshan. His mother was Sheshans daughter Ahlai. Attai was born to Ahlai and Jarha (The Egyptian servant of Sheshan). Attai was the father of Nathan **(I Chronicles 2:34-36)** Also another Attai was the son of King Rehoboam of Judah and brother of King Abija **(II Chronicles 11:17-20).** ***Meaning*** That Which Increases (At-tie) Male

AUGUSTUS An important Roman Emperor **(Luke 2:1) (Acts 25:21)** ***Meaning*** Increased and Augmented (Or-gus-tas) Male

AWAN or LULUWA The first daughter of Adam and Eve she married her brother Cain (not mentioned in the KJV) **(Genesis 39:12)** ***Meaning*** One of Assistance (Ar-one) Female

AZARIAH There are over 20 Azariahs mentioned in the bible. One was a son of Jehu and the father of Helez (From the line of Sheshan through his daughter Ahlai and his Egyptian servant Jarha **(I Chronicles 2:34-39)**. Another was a son of Zadok **(I Kings 4:2)** Another Azariah of note was a son of Ahimaaz and the father of Johanan **(I Chronicles 6:9)**. ***Meaning*** To Whom God Strengthened (Az-a-rye-ah) Male

AZUBAH The wife of Caleb her sons were Jesher, Shobab and Ardon **(1 Chr. 2:18, 19)**. There are three women called Azubah in the bible ***Meaning*** Deserted (A-Zoo-bar) Female

AZUR or AZZUR The father of Hananiah **(Jeremiah 28:1)** ***Meaning*** Helper (A-zur) Male

AZURA or AKILIA/AKELMIA or KALI AZURA The Second daughter of Adam and Eve, she married her brother Seth (not mentioned in the KJV) **(Genesis 39:12)** ***Meaning*** Blue Sky (A-zur-ra) Female

AZZAN The father of Paltiel of the tribe Issachar **(Numbers 34:26)** ***Meaning*** Their Strength (Ae-zan) Male

B

BAALAH The early name of Kiriath-Jearim ***Meaning*** Mistress **(Joshua 15:9)** (Ba-ar-la) Male/Female

BAASHA Son of Ahijah and the third King of Israel **(I Kings 15:33, I Kings 16:8)** and the father of Elah, who followed him as King **(I Kings 16:6)** ***Meaning*** He That Seeks (Ba-ar-sha) Male

BALADAN The father of the Babylonian King Merodach Baladan **(2 Kings 20:12) (Isaiah 39:1)** ***Meaning*** God Has Given a Son (Bal-a-dan) Male

BARABBAS A robber who was pardoned so that Jesus could be put to death **(Matthew 27:16-26) (Acts 3:14)** ***Meaning*** The Son of Abba or of the Father (Ba-rab-bas) Male

BARAK The son of Abinoam **(Judges 4:6)** ***Meaning*** Lightning (Ba-rack) Male

BARAKA The wife of Jared and mother of Enoch, she was the grandmother of Methuselah (not mentioned in the KJV) ***Meaning*** Blessing (Bar-rak-ka) Female

BARNABAS The surname of Joses, a Levite. His name is first on the list of prophets and teachers of the church at Antioch. Barnabas was a good man and a friend of Pauls **(Acts 4:36)** ***Meaning*** Son of Consolation and Comfort (Bar-na-bus) Male

BALTHASAR One of the three wise men, the other two were named Caspar and Melchior **(Matthew 2:1)** ***Meaning*** Protecting the King (Bal-tha-zar) Male

BARTHOLOMEW The son of Tolmai and one of the twelve Disciples also known as Nathanael **(Matthew 10:3) (Acts 1:13)** ***Meaning*** Son of a Farmer and Friend (Bar-thol-o-mew) Male

BARTIMAEUS Son of Timaeus, one of the two blind beggars of Jericho who were cured because of their strong faith in the Lord **(Mark 10:46) (Matthew 20:30)** ***Meaning*** Son of The Honourable (Bar-ti-may-us) Male

BASHAN Mentioned in the bible a few times Bashan was a city **(Genesis 14:5)** ***Meaning*** Light Soil or One of The Earth (Bash-an) Male/Female

BASHEMATH or MAHALATH A wife of Esau, daughter of Ishmael and sister of Ishmaels son Nebajoth **(Genesis 36:3)** the mother of Reuel **(Genesis 36:4)** ***Meaning*** Sweet Smelling (Bas-ee-math) Female

BATHSHEBA or BATHSHUA The daughter of Eliam **(II Samuel 11:3)** and wife of Uriah **(II Samuel 11:4-5)**. King David sent her husband Uriah out to be killed in battle **(II Samuel 11:14-17)** after Uriahs death she became one of Davids wives **(II Samuel 11:26-27)**. She became pregnant by David and the first baby boy died shortly after birth **(II Samuel 12:11-18)** but Bathsheba had more sons to David including Solomon, Nathan, Shammua and Shobab **(I Chronicles 3:5)** ***Meaning*** Daughter of Oath (Bath-she-ba) (Bath-shew-a) Female

BEERAH He was Prince of the Reubenites **(1Ch 5:6)** ***Meaning*** A Well or Fountain (Be-ee-ra) Male

BEERI A Hittite, he was father of Judith, a wife of Esau **(Genesis 26:34)** ***Meaning*** Illustrious and Well (Be-ee-ri) Male

BENAIAH He was the son of Jehoiada. As Chief Priest he remained faithful to Solomon **(1 Chr. 27:5) (2 Sam. 23:20, 21)** There are five Benaiahs mentioned in the bible. ***Meaning*** Built Up By the Lord (Ben-nye-ah) Male

BENAMMI The second son of Lot, born by Lots daughter. She got her father drunk and had intercourse with him in order to preserve his bloodline. Benammi is the founding father of the Children of Ammon until this day **(Genesis 19:31-38)** ***Meaning*** Son of My Kindred (Ben-na-mee) Male

BENJAMIN The twelfth and last born of Jacobs sons and founder of the Tribe of Israel, Benjamin. He was the second-born son of Jacobs second wife Rachel **(Genesis 35:16-18)**. Rachel was dying at the time of his birth and she named him Benoni (Son of my sorrow) but Jacob would later call him Benjamin. His brothers were Asher, Dan, Gad, Issachar, Joseph, Judah, Levi, Naphtali, Reuben, Simeon and Zebulun. His sister was Dinah. **(Genesis 35:18)** ***Meaning*** Son of my right hand (Ben-ja-min) Male

BENONI The first name given to Benjamin the twelfth son of Jacob by his mother Rachel who was dying at the time **(Genesis 35:16-18)**. Jacob would later change his name to Benjamin. ***Meaning*** Son of My Sorrow (Ben-no-nee) Male

BEOR The father of Belaam **(Numbers 22:5)** Another was the father of Bela one of the Kings of Edom **(Gen. 36:32)** ***Meaning*** A Torch Light (Be-or) Male

BERECHIAH A son of Zerubabble and grandson of Pedaiah **(1 Chronicles 3:19-20)** ***Meaning*** Blessed by the Lord (Ber-a-kee-ar) Male

BERIAH One of the sons of Asher, his sister was Serah and his brothers were Imnah, Isuah and Ishuai. He is one of the grandchildren of Jacob **(Genesis 46:17) (Numbers 26:44,45)** ***Meaning*** Gift of Brotherhood or Gift of Fellowship. Also means In Envy (Ber-rye-a) Male

BERNICE The daughter of Herod Agrippa I and sister of Agrippa II, Married to King Herod of Chalcis who was her uncle ***Meaning*** One Who Brings Victory (Ber-nee-ss) Female

BETENOS The mother of Noah and Wife of Lamech, a very important lady (not mentioned in the KJV) ***Meaning*** Belly or womb (Bet-ten-noss) Female

BETHANY The name of a town east of Jordan. Jesus slept the nights at Bethany **(Matthew 21:17, 26:6) (Mark 11:11)** ***Meaning*** House of Dates (Beth-than-ee) Female/Male

BETHER One of the four sons of Aram **(Genesis 10:23)** ***Meaning*** Division (Beth-ther) Male

BETHUEL A brother of Huz and Buz and one of the eight sons of Milcah and Nahor. He was the father of Laban and Rebekah (Isaacs wife) **(Genesis 22:23) (Genesis 22: 20-21) (Genesis 24:29, 67)** ***Meaning*** A Man of God (Beth-you-el) Male

BILDAD One of the friends who consoled Job **(Job 2:11)** ***Meaning*** The Son of Contention or Controversy (Bil-dar-d) Male

BILAH or BILHAH Rachels handmaid servant, who was given to Jacob **(Genesis 29:29)**. She was the mother of Dan and Naphtali, two of the founders of the tweleve tribes of Israel **(Genesis 30:3-8)** ***Meaning*** Timid and Bashful (Bil-ha) Female

BILSHAN The man who returned from Captivity with Zerubbabel **(Ezra 2:2) (Nehemiah 7:7)** ***Meaning*** A Man of Eloquence (Bil-sharn) Male

BIMHAL One of the sons of Japhlet from the tribe of Asher, his brothers were Ashvath and Pasach **(1Ch 7:33)** ***Meaning*** Son of Circumcision (Bim-Hal) Male

BOAZ A son of Salmon and Rachab. He was the husband of Ruth and a very wealthy man from Bethlehem **(Ruth 3:12)**. Boaz was also the name of one of the two columns in Solomons Temple (The other column was called Jachin) **(1 Kings 7:15,22)** ***Meaning*** Eager and Willing (Bo-az) Male

BUZ A brother of Huz and a son of Milcah and Nahor **(Genesis 22: 20-21)**. There are three men named Buz in the bible ***Meaning*** Contempt (Bu-zz) Male

C

CAESAR The title taken by Roman Emperors after Julius Caesar. **(John 19:15)** (See-zar) ***Meaning*** Long Haired one Male/Female

CAIAPHAS Surname of Joseph the High Priest in John the Baptist time **(Luke 3:2)** ***Meaning*** The Searcher (Kay-a-fas) Male/Female

CAIN or KAIN One of the sons of Adam and Eve and brother of Able whom he killed **(Genesis 4 :1)** Cain was a tiller of the ground ***Meaning*** Fixed or Spear/Lance (Kay-n) Male

CAINAN or KENAN A son of Enosh/Enos and the grandson of Seth. One of his sons was Mahalelel/Mahaleleel who fathered Jared who fathered Enoch in the line leading to Noah. He had a wife called Mualeleth (Not mentioned in the KJV) **(Genesis 5:9,14).** Another was the son of Arphaxad **(Luke 3:36)** ***Meaning*** Owner or Possessor (Key-nan) (Kay-nan) Male

CALEB He was one of the three sons of Hezron from the tribe of Judah. There are four Calebs in the bible **(1 Chr. 2:9)** ***Meaning*** A Dog (Kay-leb) Male

CANA A town of Galilee **(Jn 2:1,11)** ***Meaning*** Beloved (Kay-na) Female/Male

CANAAN The fourth son of Ham and Grandson of Noah, his brothers were Cush, Mizraim and Phut **(Genesis 9:22).** Canaan was the father of Sidon and Heth and is the founding ancestor of the Canaanites **(Genesis 10:15-20)** Also a land mass ***Meaning*** Humiliated or Humbled (Kay-nan) Male

CANDACE The Queen of the Ethiopians. A title that other Queens took as well **(Acts 8:27)** ***Meaning*** Splendid Dazzling Glowing and Bright (Kan-dee-s) Female

CAPHTORIM One of the seven sons of Mizraim his brothers were Casluhim, Ludim, Lehabim, Naphtuhim, Pathrusim and Anamim **(Genesis 10:13-14)** ***Meaning*** Bud (Kaf-tor-rim) Male

CAREAH or KAREAH Father of Johanan and Johnathon **(Jer 40:8)** ***Meaning*** Ice (Kar-ree-ah) Male

CARMEL A park that lay within the tribe of Asher **(1 Kings 18)** ***Meaning*** A Park or Peaceful Place (Kar-mel) Female/Male

CARMI The father of Achan from the Tribe of Judah **(Joshua 7)** ***Meaning*** My Vineyard or Lamb of The Waters (Kar-mee) Male

CARSHENA A Prince of Media and Persia **(Esther 1:14)** ***Meaning*** The Lamb (Kar-shen-a) Male

CASLUHIM One of the seven sons of Mizraim and ancestor of the Philistines his brothers were were Ludim, Lehabim, Caphtorim, Naphtuhim, Pathrusim and Anamim **(Genesis 10:13-14)** ***Meaning*** Fortified (Kas-loo-him) Male

CASPAR or GASPAR He was one of the three wisemen. The other two were called Melchior and Balthasar **(Matthew 2:1)** ***Meaning*** The Treasurer or Keeper of The Treasure (Kass-par) (Gass-par) Male

CASSIA One of the spices of anointing oil **(Exodus 30:24).** Sometimes used to scent garments ***Meaning*** Split or Divide (Kay-sha) Female/Male

CEPHAS or SIMON PETER The DiscipleSimon-Peters last name, he was the son of Jonah **(Matthew 16:16,17,18)** He had a brother called Andrew who first brought him to Jesus **(John 1:40,42)** ***Meaning*** A Rock or Stone (same as Peter) (See-fas) Male

CHARMIS A magistrate of Bethulia and the son of Melchiel **(Judith 6:15)** ***Meaning*** Of the Vine (Kar-mis) Male

CHENAANAH The father of Zedekiah **(1 Kings 22:11, 24)** ***Meaning*** A Merchant (Kena-ana) Male

CHENAIAH The Chief of the Levites **(1 Chr. 15:22)** ***Meaning*** Who the Lord Has Made (Ken-nye-ah) Male

CHIDON or NACHON NACON NODAN The owner of a thrashing-floor near which Uzzah was slain **(2 Samuel 6:6)** Also called Nachon or Nodan **(1Ch 13:9)** ***Meaning*** A Dart (Kee-don) Male

CHILEAB The second son of King David by Abigail **(II Samuel 3:3)** ***Meaning*** Protected by The Father (Kil-lee-ab) Male

CHILION A son of Naomi and Elimelech and the husband of Orpah **(Ruth 1:2)** ***Meaning*** The Pining One (Kil-lee-on) Male

CHLOE A female Christian mentioned in **(1 Cor. 1:11)** ***Meaning*** Fresh Green Color, One of Growth (Klo-wee) Female

CORNELIUS A Roman Centurion and devout man of God **(Acts 10)** ***Meaning*** Horn (Kor-nee-lee-us) Male

CLAUDIA A female Christian talked about in (**2 Timothy 4:21)** ***Meaning*** Lame (Klor-dee-a) Female

CLAUDIUS The fourth Roman Emperor that succeeded Caligula **(Acts 18:2)**. There is also a Greek man name Lysias whom assumed the name of Claudius after obtaining Roman Citizenship **(Acts 21:31-40)** ***Meaning*** Lame (Klor-dee-us) Male

CUSH One of the four sons of Ham and Grandson of Noah, his brothers were Canaan, Mizraim and Phut. Cush settled in Ethiopia and his decendants settled in Ethiopia, Libya, Eqypt and Nubia. He was the father of six sons Seba, Havilah, Sabta, Raama, Sabtecha and Nimrod (The mighty one of the earth) **(Genesis 10:6-8)** ***Meaning*** Black (Ku-sh) Male

CYRUS A King of Persia and conqueror of Babylon **(Ezra 1:1, 2)** ***Meaning*** The Sun (Sy-russ) Male

D

DAEMON From the Greek form of devil although new versions of the New Testament speak of Daemons as spiritual beings which is more like it **(Matthew 8:16, 10:1)** ***Meaning*** Possessed Super-Human Being (De-mon) or (Day-mon) Male

DALPHON A Son of Haman his brothers were Parshandatha and Aspatha **(Esther 9:7)** ***Meaning*** House of Caves (Del-fon) Male

DAMARIS A woman from Athens whom Paul converted to Christianity **(Acts 17:34)** ***Meaning*** A Heifer (Da-mar-riss) Female

DAMASCUS A City of Syria **(2 Kings 5:12)** ***Meaning*** Activity (Da-mas-kuss) Male/Female

DAN The fifth-born of Jacobs twelve sons and founder of the Tribe of ISRAEL, DAN. His biological mother was Bilah, the handmaid of Jacobs second wife Rachel (Who was barren at the time). His brothers were Asher, Benjamin, Gad, Issachar, Joseph, Judah, Levi, Naphtali, Reuben, Simeon and Zebulun. His sister was Dinah **(Genesis 30:1-6)** ***Meaning*** A Judge (d-an) Male

DANIEL King Davids second son **(1 Chr. 3:1)** Also one of the great prophets **(Daniel 1:3)** ***Meaning*** God is My Judge (Da-nee-el) Male

DANNAH A city in the mountains of Judah **(Joshua 15:49)** ***Meaning*** A Murmuring (Dar-nah) Female/Male

DAPHNE One of the suburbs of Antioch famous for its Temple of Apollo **(2 Mac 40:30)** ***Meaning*** Laurel Tree (Daf-nee) Female/Male

DARIC A Gold Coin **(Nehemiah 7:70)** ***Meaning*** Strong (Dar-rik) Male/Female

DARIUS The name of several Persian Kings (**Ezra 4:25) (Daniel 5:31) (Zech 1:1) (Haggai 1:1)** ***Meaning*** The Supporter (Da-rye-us) Male

DATHAN A son of Eliab from the tribe of Reuben. **(Numbers 16:12)** ***Meaning*** Belonging to the Fountain (Day-than) Male

DAVID The second King of the Unified Kingdom and the eighth son of Jesse. He was from the tribe of Judah. King David had lots of wives and concubines and was the father of many sons including Solomon. David was the great grandson of Ruth and Boaz. His grandfather was Obed and his father was Jesse. King David had eight brothers and two Sisters **(2 Samuel)** ***Meaning*** Beloved One (Day-vid) Male

DEACON From the Greek Diakonos **(1 Timothy 3:8)** ***Meaning*** Minister or Servant (Dee-kon) Male

DEBORAH Rebekahs nurse **(Genesis 24:59)** ***Meaning*** A Bee or Industrious (De-boor-rah) Female

DEDAN A son of Raamah and grandson of Cush **(Genesis 10:7, I Chronicles 1:9)**. Also another DEDAN was a son of Jokshan and grandson of Abraham and Ketura **(Genesis 25:3) (I Chronicles 1:32)** ***Meaning*** Low Lying Ground (Dee-dan) Male

DELILAH A Philistine woman who Samson fell madly in love with **(Judges 16:4-20)** ***Meaning*** Languishing. (Dee-lye-la) Female

DEMAS A friend of Pauls during his first imprisonment in Rome **(Philemon 1:24) (Col. 4:14)** ***Meaning*** Popular (Dee-mass) Male

DEMETRIUS There are three Demetrius spoken of in the bible one was a King **(Acts 19:24)** and **(3 John 1:12)** ***Meaning*** Lover of The Earth and Follower of the Greek Goddess of Harvest (Dee-mee-tree-us) Male

DIANA See Artemis ***Meaning*** Devine One

DIDYMUS or THOMAS One of the twelve dicisiples **(Matthew 10:3 Mark 3:18 Luke 6:15)** ***Meaning*** Double (Did-dee-mus) Male

DIKLAH One of the thirteen sons of Joktan his brothers were Almodad, Sheleph, Hazarmaveth, Jerah, Hadoram, Uzal, Ebal, Abimael, Sheba, Ophir, Havilah and Jobab **(Genesis 10:25-30)**. Arabs from the line of Shem ***Meaning*** Palm Tree (Dick-la) Male

DINAH There were two Dinahs in the Bible. One was the daughter of Jacob born to Jacobs first wife Leah **(Genesis 30:20-21)**. She was kidnapped by Shechem. Shechem raped Dinah and then had her marriage arranged to himself. Later two of Dinahs brothers (Levi and Simeon) set about to revenge there sisters misfortune, they killed Shechem. Her brothers were two of the founding members of the twelve tribes of Israel. Her brothers were Issachar, Judah, Levi, Reuben, Simeon and Zebulun (By her mother Leah) and Asher and Gad (By Leahs haidmaid Zilpah). Her Aunt Rachel had Joseph and Benjamin (By her father Jacob) and Dan and Naphtali (Were born by Rachels handmaid Bilhah) **(Genesis 34) (Genesis 34:1-2)**. Another Dinah was the wife of Mahaleleel (not mentioned in the KJV) ***Meaning*** Vindicated One or Justified One (Dye-nah) Female

DIONYSIUS One of the men that Paul converted to Christianity at Athens **(Acts 17:34)**. It is also the name of the Greek God of Wine ***Meaning*** Devine (Dye-a-nish-yus) Male/Female

DISHAN He was a son of Seir duke of Edom his siblings were Shobal, Zibeon, Anah, Dishon, Ezer, Lotan and his sister Timna **(Genesis 36:20)** ***Meaning*** Antelope (De-shan) Male

DISHON Another of the sons of Seir Duke of Edom his siblings were Dishan, Shobal, Zibeon, Anah, Ezer, Lotan and his sister Timna **(Genesis 36:20)** ***Meaning*** Ashes (De-shawn) Male

DODAI One of Davids captains **(1 Chr. 27:4)** ***Meaning*** Loving (Doe-die) Male

DODANIM or RODANIM One of the four sons of Javan **(Genesis 10:4)** ***Meaning*** Leader (Doe-da-nim) Male

DORCAS or TABITHA A Christian widow at Joppa who Peter restored to life **(Acts 9:36-41)** ***Meaning*** A Gazelle (Door-kas) Female

DRUSILLA The wife of Felix she left her husband the King of Emesa to become Felix wife **(Acts 24:24)** ***Meaning*** Watered by The Dew (Drew-sil-la) Female

DUMAH Fourth of the twelve sons of Ishmael his brothers were Nebaioth, Kedar, Adbeel, Mibsam, Mishma, Massa, Hadad, Tema, Jetur, Naphish and Kedemah **(Genesis 25) (I Chronicles 1:29-30)** ***Meaning*** Silence (Due-mar) Male

E

EBAL One of the thirteen sons of Joktan his brothers were Almodad, Sheleph, Hazarmaveth, Jerah, Hadoram, Uzal, Diklah, Abimael, Sheba, Ophir, Havilah and Jobab. **(Genesis 10:25-30**). ***Meaning*** Ancient and Stony (Ee-ball) Male

EBER Son of Shem and also father of Joktan and Peleg **(Genesis 10:21-25)** ***Meaning*** Beyond (Ee-ber) Male

EDEN The garden in which Adam and Eve first lived **(Genesis 2:8)** ***Meaning*** Delightful (Ee-den) Male/Female

EDER The second of the three sons of Mushi **(1 Chr. 23:23)** ***Meaning*** Flock (Ee-der) Male

EDOM The name given to Esau **(Genesis 25:30)** ***Meaning*** Red (Ee-dom) Male

EDNA The wife of Raguel and mother of Sarah who later married Tobias **(Tobias 7:2)**. There were two other Ednas in the bible, one was the wife of Enoch (The man who walked with God, Enoch was Methuselahs father). The other was the wife of Methuselah, the man who lived 969 years. Methuselah married a woman with the same name as his mother (Neither of Seths decendants named Edna are mentioned in the KJV) ***Meaning*** A Pleasure and Delight (Ed-na) Female

EDREI One of the towns of the Kingdom of Bashan **(Joshusa 12:4, 5)** ***Meaning*** Might and Strength (Ed-re-eye) Male/Female

EGLAH One of Davids wives and mother of Ithream **(2 Samuel 3:5) (1 Chr. 3:3)** ***Meaning*** A Heifer (Egg-la) Female

EGLON A King of Moab **(Judges 3:12)** ***Meaning*** A Bullock (Egg-lon) Male

EHUD Benjamins great-grandson **(1 Chr. 7:10)** ***Meaning*** Union (Ee-hud) Male

ELAH A King of Israel **(1Kings 16:8)** There are five Elahs in the bible ***Meaning*** Strong as an Oak and Strength (Ee-la) Male

ELAM One of the five sons of Shem. Shem was Noahs grandson. His brothers were Asshur, Arphaxahad, Lud and Aram **(Genesis 10:1,22)** ***Meaning*** Highland (Ee-lam) Male

ELASA or ELASAH The son of Shaphan **(Jeremiah 29:3)** ***Meaning*** God Made (El-a-sa) Male

ELDAAH A son of Midian and grandson of Abraham and Ketura **(Genesis 25:4) (I Chronicles 1:33)** ***Meaning*** Knowlegde of God (El-da-ah) Male

ELDAD One of the elders whom Moses appointed **(Numbers 11:26, 27)** ***Meaning*** Whom God Loved or Favoured by God (El-dad) Male

ELEALEH A city near Jordan part of the tribe of Reuben **(Numbers 32:3, 37)** ***Meaning*** God Has Ascended (El-ee-aye-la) Female/Male

ELEASAH A son of Helez and father of Sisamai **(I Chronicles 2:34-40)** ***Meaning*** Whom God Has Made (El-ee-aye-sa) Male

ELEAZAR The third son of Aaron **(Exodus 6:23)** ***Meaning*** God Has Helped (El-ee-aye-zar) Male

ELHANAN A warrior of the time of King David **(2 Samuel 21:19)** ***Meaning*** One to Whom God Has Graciously Bestowed (El-hay-nan) Male

ELI A High Priest of Shiloh **(1 Samuel 1:3, 9)** ***Meaning*** Ascent or Ascend (Ee-lye) Male

ELIAB Firstborn son of Jesse and brother of King David **(I Samuel 17:13-14) (I Samuel 16:5).** There are four Eliabs in the bible one was the father of Dathan and Abiram ***Meaning*** God is My Father (Ee-lye-ab) Male

ELIADA A son of King David **(II Samuel 5:13-16)** ***Meaning*** Who God Cares For (El-lye-a-da) Male

ELIAKIM or JEHOIAKIM A King of Judah and second son of King Josiah, his mother was Zebudah and his brother was Neco **(2 Kings 23:36)**. Father of Jehoiachin and Zedekiah **(II Kings 24:6)** ***Meaning*** Who God Will Raise Up (Ee-lye-a-kim) (Je-hoy-a-kim) Male

ELIAM The wife of Uriah **(2 Samuel 11:3)** ***Meaning*** Gods People or One of Gods People (Ee-lye-am) Female

ELIAS The Greek form of ELIJAH a great prophet **(Matthew 11:14)** ***Meaning*** Whose God is Jehovah or Whose God is Lord of All (Ee-lye-as) Male

ELIASHIB The son of Joiakim and father of Joiada **(Nehemiah 12:10)** There are two Eliashibs in the bible ***Meaning*** Who God Will Restore (Ee-lye-shib) Male

ELIAZER A son of Aaron by Elisheba **(Exodus 6:23)** and ancestor of a Priestly line **(I Chronicles 24:1-4)** ***Meaning*** The Most Emminent (El-lee-a-zer) Male

ELIATHAH One of the fourteen sons of Heman **(1 Chr. 25:4).** ***Meaning*** To whom God Will Come (Ee-lye-a-thah) Male

ELIDAD Chief of the tribe of Benjamin **(Numbers 34:21)** ***Meaning*** Who God Has Loved (Ee-lye-dad) Male

ELIEL A Chief of Manasseh **(1 Chr. 5:24)** There are three ELIELS in the bible ***Meaning*** To whom God is Mighty (Ee-lye-el) Male

ELIEZER The second-born son of Moses and Zipporah. **(Exodus 18:4)** There are six ELIEZER in the Bible ***Meaning*** God is His Helper (El-i-ee-zer) Male

ELIHU The son of Barachel and friend of Job **(Job 32:2)** ***Meaning*** Whose God He Is (Ee-lye-who) Male

ELIJAH *see* ELIAS A great Prophet **(Matthew 11:14)** ***Meaning*** Whose God is Jehovah Lord of All (Ee-lye-jah) Male

ELIKA One of Davids warriors **(2 Samuel 23:25)** ***Meaning*** God is His Rejector (Ee-lye-ka) Male

ELIMELECH Husband of Naomi and father-in-law of Ruth **(Ruth 1,3)** ***Meaning*** God is His King (Ee-lim-el-leck) Male

ELIPHAZ Son of Esau by Adah **(Genesis 36:10)** ***Meaning*** God is His Strength (El-ee-faz) Male

ELIPHELET A son of King David **(II Samuel 5:13-16)**. There are three ELIPHELETS in the bible. Another is the son of Adonikam who had 667 children, Eliphelet brothers were Shemaiah and Jeiel. **(Ezra 8:13)** ***Meaning*** God is My Deliverance (Ee-lif-a-let) Male

ELISHA A great Prophet and the son of Shaphat of Abel-mehola. He was the disciple of Elijah **(1 Kings 19:16-19)** ***Meaning*** God is Salvation (Ee-lye-sha) Male

ELISHAH One of the four sons of Javan **(Genesis 10:4)** ***Meaning*** Lamb of God (Ee-lye-shar) Male

ELISHAMA A son of King David by an unnamed wife **(II Samuel 5:13-16) (I Chronicles 3:8, 14:7)** Another was the son of Shallum and the father of Jekamiah. **(1Ch 2:41)** Another was the grandson of Laadan and son of Ammihud **(1Ch 7:26) (Numbers 1:10 2:18)** ***Meaning*** Who God Hears (Ee-lish-a-ma) Male

ELISHEBA A daughter of Aminidab and the wife of Aaron, she had four sons to Aaron **(Genesis 6:23)** ***Meaning*** God is Her Oath (Ee-lish-a-ba) Female

ELISHUA A son of King David by an unnamed wife **(II Samuel 5:13-16)** ***Meaning*** God is Salvation (El-ee-shoo-a) Male

ELKANAH The second son of Korah **(Ex. 6:24)** ***Meaning*** God Has Created. (El-ka-na) Male

ELNATHAN The father of Nehushta (The wife of King Eliakim of Judah) **(2 Kings 24:8)** ***Meaning*** Who God Has Given (El-Nay-than) Male

ELON A Hittite, father of Adah **(Genesis 36:2) (Genesis 4:17)** Elon is listed as father of Bashemath (The wife of Esau). Also a Girls name ***Meaning*** God Loves Me (Ee-lon) Male/Female

ELYMAIS A place in Persia, Elam Minor **(Tobias 2:10)** ***Meaning*** High Place or Lofty One (El-ee-may-is) Female/Male

EMMANUEL IMMANUEL **(Matthew 1:23)** ***Meaning*** God is with us

ENOCH The Eldest son of Cain (Adam and Eves third son) and father of Irad, Enoch (not the father of Methuselah) was the Grandfather of Mehujael **(Genesis 4:16-18)**. There are two Enochs in the bible the other one is from the line of Seth. Seths son Enosh fathered

Kenan/Cainan who fathered Mahalalel who fathered Jared who fathered Enoch (The 7th decendant from Adam) Enoch walked with God and he fathered Methuselah (The longest living man 969 years) Methuselah fathered Lamech who fathered Noah. Enoch had a wife called Edna (not mentioned in the KJV) ***Meaning*** Initiated One (Ee-nock) Male

ENOS or ENOSH A son of Seth and the father of Cainan, he had a wife called Noam (not mentioned in the KJV) **(Genesis 5:6, 9-11)** ***Meaning*** Man (Ee-noss) Male

EPAPHRAS Pauls friend and a faithful follower of Christ **(Col. 1:7, 4:12)** ***Meaning*** Lovely (Ee-pa-fras)

EPHAH A son of Midian, and grandson of Abraham **(Genesis 25:4, I Chronicles 1:33).** Another was a decendant of Caleb and the Son of Jahdai, whose brothers were Jotham, Regem, Geshan, Pelet and Shaaph **(1Ch 2:47)** ***Meaning*** Gloom (Ee-fa) Male

EPHER A son Midian and Abrahams son by Ketura **(Genesis 25:4) (I Chronicles 1:33)** ***Meaning*** A Calf (Ee-fer) Male

EPHLAL A son of Zabad and father of Obed (In the lineage of Sheshan through his daughter, Ahlai and his Egyptian servant Jarha **(I Chronicles 2:34-37)**. ***Meaning*** Judgement (Ef-lal) Male

EPHRAIM The second of Josephs sons (Joseph and his eleven brothers founded the Twelve Tribes of Israel) and Grandson of Joacob. Ephraim went on to found his own Israelite tribe EPHRAIM. His Brother Manasseh founded the Israelite tribe MANASSEH **(Genesis 41:52)** ***Meaning*** Bountiful and Fruitful one (Ee-fra-im) Male

EPHRON Abraham was buried in a field belonging to Ephron his fathers name was Zohar **(Genesis 25:8-10)** ***Meaning*** Like a Fawn (Ef-ron) Male

ESAU Rebekahs first-born twin son **(Genesis 25:25)** ***Meaning*** Rough (Ee-saw) Male

ESHEAN A mountinous place in Judah **(Josh.15:52)** ***Meaning*** Held up (Ess-she-an) Female/Male

ESROM see HEZRON ***Meaning*** Enclosed (Hez-ron or Ez-rom) Male

ESTHER The Queen of Ahasuerus and the heroine of the book of Esther **(Esther 1)**. Esthers real name was Hadassah before entering the royal harem ***Meaning*** Hidden in Hebrew and Myrtle Blossom Star in Persian (Ess-ter) Female

ETHAN A man of wisdom of the tribe of Levi **(1 Kings 4:31).** He is named as the author of the 89th Psalm. His father was Kushaiah/Kishi singer in the temple during King Davids reign ***Meaning*** Firm (Ee-than) Male

ETHBAAL Father of Jezebel and the King of the Zidonians **(1Ki 16:31)** ***Meaning*** Toward an Idol or with Baal the Idol Worshipped (Eth-ba-al) Male

EUNICE A Jewish Woman from Galatia her son was Timothy and hermother was Lois **(Acts 16:1)** ***Meaning*** The Happy Conquerer (U-niss) Female

EVE The mother of all. Adams wife and the first women of earth **(Genesis 1)** ***Meaning*** Lifegiver and To live (Ee-ve) Female

EZEKIEL One of the great prophets, the son of Buzi (The priest) and the book that bears his name EZEKIEL **(Ezekiel 1:3)** ***Meaning*** God Will Strengthen (Ee-zee-kay-el) Male

EZER Another of the sons of Seir Duke of Edom his siblings were Dishan, Shobal, Zibeon, Anah, Dishon, Ezer, Lotan and his sister Timna **(Genesis 36:20)** ***Meaning*** A Great Help or A Great Treasure (Ee-zer) Male

EZRA A priest and scribe the book bears his name **(Ezra 7:12 Nehemiah 8:9)** Ezra was son of Saraiah and brother of Jehozadak **(Ezra 7:1) (I Chronicles 6:14)**. He led the people back from exile in Babylon. ***Meaning*** Helper (Ez-ra) Male

F

FAITH A belief that certain things and statements are truths **(Phil. 1:27)** ***Meaning*** Belief (F-aye-th) Female/Male

FELIX A Roman from Judea and husband of Drusilla he allured her to leave her husband, the King of Emesa to become his wife **(Acts 24:25)** ***Meaning*** Happy (Fee-lix) Male

FISHER The lord said thou shalt be fishers of men **(Matthew 4:19) (Mark 1:17)** ***Meaning*** A Fisherman or Provider (Fi-sher) Male

FULLER The art of whitening clothes a very auspicious act. Jesus garments were made white with this process at his transfiguration **(Mark 9:3)** ***Meaning*** To Whiten or Whiteness (Full-er) Male/Female

G

GAAL Son of Obed from the city of Shechem **(Judges 9:26)** ***Meaning*** Loathing (Gay-al) Male

GABAEL Son or brother of Gabrias **(Tobias 1:4)** ***Meaning*** Good (Gab-aye-el) Male

GABRIAS The father or brother of Gabael. Tobiah was sent to get his fathers money back from Gabrias **(Tobias 4:20)** ***Meaning*** Good (Gay-bree-ass) Male

GABRIEL The name of the angel who was sent to help Daniel **(Daniel 8:16)** ***Meaning*** Champion of God and God is Strong (Gay-bree-el) Male/Female

GAD The seventh son of Jacobs twelve sons born to Zilpah the handmaiden of Jacobs wife Leah and founder of the Tribe of ISRAEL, GAD. His brothers were Asher, Benjamin, Dan, Issachar, Joseph, Judah, Levi, Naphtali, Reuben, Simeon and Zebulun. His sister was Dinah. **(Genesis 30:9-11)** ***Meaning*** Troop (G-ad) Male

GADARA A Greek city southeast of the Sea of Galilee and Capital of the Roman province of Peraea **(Mark 5:1)** ***Meaning*** Wall or Surrounding or Mountain top (Gad-dar-a) Female/Male

GADI or GADDI or GADDIEL Father of King Menahem of Israel. One of the twelve spies sent by Moses to spy on the land, he represented the tribe of Zebulum **(Numbers 13:10,11)** ***Meaning*** One of Fortune (Gad-dee) Male

GAHAM Son of Nahor, Abrahams brother by his concubine Reumah **(Genesis 22:24)** ***Meaning*** Burner (Gay-am) Male

GAHAR One of the Chiefs of Nethinim **(Ezra 2:47)** ***Meaning*** Place to Lurk (Gay-har) Male

GAIUS A Macedonian companion of Pauls **(Romans 16:23)** There are three Gaius mentioned in the bible ***Meaning*** Joyful or Rejoicing (Gay-us) Male

GALLIO The elder brother of Seneca the philosopher **(Acts 18:12)** ***Meaning*** One Who Suckles or Lves on Milk (Ga-lio) Male

GAMALIEL A chief of the tribe of Manasseh at the census at Sinai **(Numbers 1:10)** The other Gamaliel mentioned in the bible was the son of the Rabbi Simeon ***Meaning*** Reward of God. (Gay-may-lee-el) Male

GARRISON A military post as spoken of in Samuel **(1 Sam. 13:23)** ***Meaning*** A Place One Stands (Gari-son) Male/Female

GASPAR or CASPER One of the three wisemen **(Matthew 2:1)** ***Meaning*** The Treasurer or Keeper of The Treasure (Cass-par) (Gass-par) Male

GEDALIAH The son of Jeduthum **(1 Chr. 25:3)**. There are two GEDALIAHS in the bible. Another was a son of Ahikam, he was named by Nebuchadnezzar Governor of Judah **(2 Kings 25:22)** ***Meaning*** Made Great by The Lord (Ged-a-lye-ah) Male

GEHAZI A servant of Elisha who turned bad and extorted money from him **(2 Kings 4:13**) ***Meaning*** Valley of Vision (Gee-hay-zye) Male

GEMARIAH A Levite and son of Shaphan **(2 Kings 22:12)** There are two GEMARIAHS in the bible. The other was the son of Hilikiah, he was an officer of King Zedekiah **(Jeremiah 29:3)** ***Meaning*** The Lord Has Made Perfect (Gee-ma-rye-ah) Male

GERSHOM One was the firstborn son of Moses and Zipporah **(Exodus 2:22)** There are four Gershoms mentioned in the bible another is a descendant of Aaron **(Ezra 8:2)** ***Meaning*** Expulsion (Ger-shom) Male

GERSHON The eldest of Levis three sons. Gershon had two sons Libni and Shimei **(Genesis 46:11)** ***Meaning*** To expel (Ger-shon) Male

GESHAN A decendant of Caleb and the Son of Jahdai whose brothers were Jotham, Regem, Pelet, Ephah and Shaaph **(1Ch 2:47)** ***Meaning*** Hard (Ge-shan) *G as in Get.* Male

GIDEON or JERUBBAAL Son of Joash, the Abiezrite **(Judges 6:11)** Gideon had seventy sons to many wives **(Judges 8:30)** including Abimelech, after Gideons death Abimelech killed all but one of his half-brothers (he did not kill Jotham) **(Joshua 9:5)**. He reigned for three years over Israel **(Joshua 9:22).** ***Meaning*** Mighty Warrior (Gid-dee-on) Male

GINATH The father of Tibni **(1 Kings 16:21)** ***Meaning*** A Garden (Gye-nath) Male

GOLIATH There are two giants named Goliath in the bible one more famous than the other. One fought the armies of Israel but was eventually slain by David with a stone and a sling **(Samuel 17:4)**. The other GOLIATH was slain by Elhanan (he may have been called Lahmi as well) **(2 Samuel 21:19)** ***Meaning*** Great One (Go-lye-ath) Male

GOMER One of the seven sons of Japheth and the father of Ashkenaz, Riphath and Togarmah **(Genesis 10:2-3).** Another GOMAR is the daughter of Diblaim who became the wife of Hosea. They had three children, two sons named Jezreel and Lo-ammi and a daughter named Lo-ruhamah **(Hosea 1:3)** ***Meaning*** Vanishing (Go-mer) Female/Male

GRACE Favour of Etiquette and Kindness **(Proverbs 1:9)** ***Meaning*** Beauty and Charm of Form and A Gift (Gray-ss) Female

H

HABAKKUK The eighth of the twelve Prophets **(Habakkuk 1)** ***Meaning*** To Embrace and One Who Embraces (Ha-baa-cook) Male

HACALIAH The father of Nehemiah **(Nehemiah 1:1)** ***Meaning*** Waiting on Jehovah, God, Yahweh (Hack-a-lye-a) Male

HADAD or HADAR One of the twelve sons of Ishmael his brothers were Nebaioth, Kedar, Adbeel, Mibsam, Mishma, Dumah, Massa, Tema, Jetur, Naphish and Kedemah **(Genesis 25)** **(I Chronicles 1:29-30)** ***Meaning*** Brave One (Ha-dad) (Ha-dar) Male

HADAREZER or HADADEZER The name given to Hadadezer **(2 Samuel 8:3-12)** ***Meaning*** Of His Help, Of Gods Help (Had-a-ree-zer) (Had-a-dee-zer) Male

HADASHAH One of the cities of Judah **(Joshua 15:37)** ***Meaning*** New (Ha-da-shar) Female/Male

HADASSAH The Jewish name of Esther **(Esther 2:7)** ***Meaning*** Myrtle and Evergreen (Ha-dar-sa) Female

HADORAM One of the thirteen sons of Joktan his brothers were Almodad, Sheleph, Hazarmaveth, Jerah, Uzal, Diklah, Ebal, Abimael, Sheba, Ophir, Havilah and Jobab. **(Genesis 10:25-30).**There are three HADORAMS mentioned in the bible ***Meaning*** One Whom is Exalted (Ha-Door-am) Male

HAGAR She was an Egyptian servant of Sarah (Sarai, Abrahams wife). Because Sarah was unable to have children she gave Hagar to her husband Abraham to bear his child. Hagar bore

Ishmael and Sarah told Abram (Abrahams name at the time) to drive them from the country **(Genesis 16:1-2, 6)** Ishmael went on to become the founder of a very great nation **(Genesis 17:20)** ***Meaning*** Of Flight (Hay-gar) Female

HAGGI One of the sons of Gad **(Genesis 46:16)** ***Meaning*** Festive One, Joyous One, Dancing One (Hag-eye) Male

HAGGAI One of the prophets **(Ezra 6:14)** ***Meaning*** Festive, Joyous and Merry **(Hag-eye)** Male

HAGGITH A wife of King David and the mother of Davids fourth son Adonijah **(2 Samuel 3:4)** ***Meaning*** The Dancer (Ha-gith) Female

HAIL A salutation and best wishes **(Luke 1:8)** ***Meaning*** To Rejoice (Hay-el) Male/Female

HALLEL The name given to a group of Psalms **(Psalms 113-118)** ***Meaning*** To Praise (Ha-lel) Male/Female

HAM The second of the three sons of Noah, his brothers were Japheth and Shem. Hams descendants became the people of Africa and parts of Arabia. His sons were Cush, Mizraim, Phut and Canaan **(Genesis 5:32)**. ***Meaning*** Hot or Black (Ha-m) Male

HAMAN Prime Minister of Persia he served King Ahasuerus he plotted against Esther and was impeded by Esther and Mordecai and eventually hanged **(Esther 3:1,2,3,4,5)** ***Meaning*** Magnificent and Noisey and Heard by all (Hay-man) Male

HAMMEDATHA The son of Haman **(Esther 3:1)** ***Meaning*** He That Troubles Law (Ham-ma-day-tha) Male

HAMMURABI The sixth King of Babylon **(Genesis 14)** ***Meaning*** Exalted Prince (Ham-mur-ra-bee) Male

HAMMOLEKETH A daughter of Machir and sister of Gilead **(I Chronicles 7:14-18)** and the mother of Abiezer, Mahalah and Ishod. There is no mention of her husband in the bible **(I Chronicles 7:18)**. ***Meaning*** Mountain of Strength (Ham-mo-lee-keth)

HAMOR The Hivite father of Shechem (Shesham raped Jacobs daughter Dinah, and made her his wife. He was slain along with other Hivites by Jacobs sons Levi and Simeon). **(Genesis 34)** ***Meaning*** An Ass (Hay-mor) Male

HAMUL Son of Perez and grandson of Judah **(Genesis 46:12) (Numbers 26:21) (1 Chronicles 2:5)** ***Meaning*** Merciful and Godly (Hay-mul) Male

HAMUTAL The daughter of Jeremiah and the wife of King Josiah of Judah. She had two sons, King Jehoahaz II and King Zedekiah **(2 Kings 23:36 24:18)** ***Meaning*** Kinsmen of The Dew (Ha-moo-tal) Female

HANNAH The mother of Samuel, her story can be found in the first book of Samuel **(1Samuel 1:1,18)** ***Meaning*** Gracious and Merciful One and Favourable one (Han-na) Female

HANAMEL or HANAMEEL A cousin of the prophet Jeremiah **(Jeremiah 32:1)** ***Meaning*** Grace From God (Han-a-mel) Male

HANANI The father of the prophet Jehu **(1 Kings 16:1)** ***Meaning*** My Grace and Mercy (Ha-nay-nee) Male

HANANIAH The son of Zerubabbel and grandson of Pedaiah **(I Chronicles 3:19-21)**. ***Meaning*** Gracious Gift of The Lord (Han-na-nye-a) Male

HARAN His father was Terah. Haran was Abrahams brother and he was the father of Lot, Iscah and Milcah **(Genesis 11:26-29)** ***Meaning*** Roads and Mountaineer (Har-ran) Male

HASADIAH A son of Zerubabble and grandson of Pedaiah **(1 Chronicles 3:19-20)** ***Meaning*** Mercy of the Lord and Favoured by Jehovah (Has-a-dye-a) Male

HASHABIAH There are about nine males named Hashabiah in the bible. A Merarite Levite **(1 Chronicles 6:45, 9:14)**. A son of Jeduthun **(Chronicles 25:3,19)**. A son of Kemuel **(Chronicles 26:30)**. One of the Chief Levites **(2 Chr. 35:9)**. ***Meaning*** Regarded by Jehovah in the Estimation of the Lord (Hash-a-bye-a)

HASHUBA A son of Zerubabbel and grandson of Pedaiah and decendant of King David **(1 Chronicles 3:19-20)** ***Meaning*** One of Thought and Estimation (Hash-shoo-ba)

HASHEM or HASHUM He stood on Ezras left hand while he read the law **(Nehemiah 8:4)** ***Meaning*** Opulent One and Silenced (Hash-shem) Male

HAVILAH One of the six sons of Cush (Ethiopian) his brothers were Seba, Havilah, Sabta, Raama, Sabtecha and Nimrod (The mighty one) **(Genesis 10:7)**. The other Havilah in the bible is one of the thirteen sons of Joktan his brothers were Almodad, Sheleph, Hazarmaveth, Jerah, Hadoram, Uzal, Diklah, Ebal, Abimael, Sheba, Ophir, and Jobab **(Genesis 10:25-30)**. ***Meaning*** He That Suffers and Brings Forth (Have-ill-la) Male

HAZAEL An officer of Ben-Hadad II a Syrian **(1 Kings 19:15)** ***Meaning*** Whom That God Beholds (Hay-za-eel) Male

HAZARMAVETH or HADRAMAWETH One of the thirteen sons of Joktan his brothers were Almodad, Sheleph, Jerah, Hadoram, Uzal, Diklah, Ebal, Abimael, Sheba, Ophir, Havilah and Jobab **(Genesis 10:25-30)**. ***Meaning*** Dwelling Court of Sleep (Haz-ar-mar-veth) or (Had-dra-mar-weth) Male

HELEZ A son of Azariah and father of Eleasah (In the line of Sheshan through his daughter Ahlai and his Egyptian servant Jarha) **(I Chronicles 2:34-39)**. ***Meaning*** Armed and Strong (Hell-lez) Male

HENOCH or ENOCH A son Midian and grandson of Abraham by Ketura **(Genesis 25:4) (I Chronicles 1:33)** ***Meaning*** The Initiated One (Hen-nock) Male

HEPHZIBAH Wife of King Hezekiah of Judah and mother of King Manesseh **(II Kings 21:1)** ***Meaning*** My Delight is in Her (Hef-zi-bar) Female

HERODIAN or HERODION A Christian man of Rome who Paul salutes and calls kinsman **(Romans 16:11)** ***Meaning*** The Son of Juno (He-row-dee-an) (He-row-dee-on) Male

HERODIAS The daughter of Aristobulus and Bernice married to Herod Philip I (**Matthew 14:3-11) (Mark 6:17-28) (Luke 3:19)** ***Meaning*** One Who Watches Over (He-row-dee-as) Female

HETH The second-born son of Canaan and a grandson of Noah **(Genesis 10:1,15)** ***Meaning*** Dread and Fear (Heh-th) Male

HEZEKIAH A King of Judah. The son of King Ahaz, whom he succeeded to be King of Judah **(2 Kings 18:1 2) (Chr. 29:1)** ***Meaning*** To Who Jehovah Has Strengthened (Hez-ee-kye-ah) Male

HEZRON or ESROM The son of Pharez and grandson of Judah from the line of King David, the father of Ram (Amram) **(Genesis 46:12) (Ruth 4:18-19)**. He was also the father of Caleb (Chelubai) and Jerahmeel **(I Chronicles 2:9, 2:18)**. Hw then married a daughter of Machir and had another son named Segub **(I Chronicles 2:21)**. After his death his wife Abiah gave birth to another son named Ashur **(I Chronicles 2:24.)** ***Meaning*** Enclosed (Hez-ron) Male

HILKIAH The son of Shallum and the father of Azariah from the Levite line **(I Chronicles 6:13)** ***Meaning*** God is My Peace (Hill-kye-a) Male

HOGLAH One of the five daughters of Zelophehad her sisters were Mahlah, Noah, Tirazh and Milcah **(Numbers 26:33)** ***Meaning*** His Dance or The Lords Dance (Ho-gla) Female

HOSANNA An invocation that the crowd chanted to Jesus on his entry into Jerusalem **(Psalms 118:25) (Matthew 21:9) (Mark 11:9)** ***Meaning*** Save We Beseech Auspiciously, Favourably Inclined (Ho-sar-na) Male/Female

HOSHAMA A son of King Jehoiachin of Judah **(1 Chr 3:18)** ***Meaning*** Whom God Hears (Ho-shar-ma) Male

HOSHEA The King of Ephraim in Davids time **(1 Chr. 27:20)**. Also the last King of Israel **(Isaiah 7:16)** Also see JOSHUA/HOSHEA namesake of the book of Joshua, an old testament book about Canaan and the sharing of territory between the twelve tribes of Israel. Joshua is the son of Nun from the tribe of Ephraim **(Numbers 13:8)**. His birth name was Hoshea but was changed later by Moses to Joshua, he became Moses successor **(Numbers 13:16)** ***Meaning*** Saviour and Deliverer of The People (Ho-say-ah) Male

HOSEA A well known Hebrew prophet, the son of Beeri and friend of Isaiah. The first biblical book in the Minor Prophets range **(Hosea 1:1)**. He was married to Gomer and had three children, two sons Jezreel and Lo-ammi and a daughter Lo-ruhamah ***Meaning*** Salvation (Ho-see) Male

HUL The second son of Aram and the grandson of Shem, He was the great grandson of Adam and Eve **(Genesis 10:23)**. ***Meaning*** A Circle (Hull) Male

HURAI One of Davids heros from the valley of Mount Gaash **(1 Chr. 11:32)**. ***Meaning*** Linen Textile Weaver (Hu-rye) Male

HUSHAI One of King Davids councilors and friends **(1 Chr. 27:33)** ***Meaning*** Quick and Hastening and Silent One (Hu-shy) Male

HUSHAM A King of Edom **(Genesis 36:34) (1Chron 1:45)** ***Meaning*** Quick and Hastening and silent (Hush-am) Male

HUZ The first-born son of Milcah and Nahor (Milcah was actually his cousin by his fathers brother) **(Genesis 22: 20-21)**. ***Meaning*** Fasten Council or Secure Council (Huzz) Male

HYACINTH or JACINTH A precious stone of a pure orange color **(Exodus 28:19) (Revelations 21:20)**. ***Meaning*** Precious Gem (Hya-sinth) or (Jay-sinth) Female/Male

I

IBHAR A son of King David born to an unnamed wife in Jerusalem **(II Samuel 5:13-16)** ***Meaning*** He That is Chosen by God (Ib-car) Male

IBZAN The tenth judge of Israel who ruled for seven years **(Judges 12:8,10)**. ***Meaning*** Illustrious One (Ib-zawn) Male

IGAL One was a son of Shecaniah **(1 Chron 2:22)**. Another Igal was the son of Nathan **(2 Samuel 23:36)**. And yet another was a son of Josephs **(Numbers 13:7)** ***Meaning*** He Redeems (Ee-gawl) Male

IMMER The father of Pashur **(Jeremiah 20:1)** ***Meaning*** Saying Aloud or Speaking Like a Lamb (Ee-mer)

IMNAH or JIMNAH A son of Asher from the tribe of Asher, his grandfather was Jacob and his brothers were Isuah, Ishuai and Beriah he also had a sister named Serah **(Genesis 46:17)** ***Meaning*** Right Hand Man and Preparing (Im-nar) (Jim-nar) Male

IRAD The son of Enoch and the father of Mehujael from the linage of Cain **(Genesis 4:16-18)** ***Meaning*** A Fleet (Ee-rad) Male

ISAAC The only son finally born to Sarah who was ninety years old at the time. Abraham his father was one hundred years old. Sarah was the one with whom God established his covenant **(Genesis 17:19)**. Abraham offered Isaac up as a sacrifice to God on a mountain in Moriah, because of his devotion to God he did not have to sacrifice him in the end **(Genesis 22)**. Isaacs wife was Rebekah, they had twin sons Jacob and Esau **(Genesis 25:20,26)**. ***Meaning*** He Will Laugh (Eye-zak) Male

ISAIAH The son of Amoz, The book of ISAIAH bears his name. He was a prophet for sixty years or more **(Isaiah 1:1, 2:1)**. ***Meaning*** The Salvation of Jehovah (Eye-zye-ah) Male

ISCAH A daughter of Haran (Abrahams brother) and sister of Milcah and Lot **(Genesis 11:29)**. ***Meaning*** To Watch or Observant One (Isk-car) Female

ISHBAK A son of Abraham by his concubine Ketura **(Genesis 25:1-2) (I Chronicles 1:32)** and brother of Zimran, Jokshan, Medan, Midian and Shuah ***Meaning*** One Who Leaves (Ish-Back) Male

ISHI Son of Appaim and father of Sheshan **(I Chronicles 2:31)** ***Meaning*** He Saves Me or The Lord Saves Me (Ish-ee) Male

ISHMAEL There were two Ishmaels in the bible of note. One was a son of Abraham (By Sarahs Egyptian handmaid Hagar). Although he and his mother Hagar were driven away from Abrahams household by Sarah, God promised Abraham that Ishmael would be the founder of a great nation, and he was. Ishmael had twelve sons there names were Nebaioth, Kedar, Adbeel, Mibsam, Mishma, Dumah, Massa, Hadad, Tema, Jetur, Naphish and Kedemah **(Genesis 25)**. The other Ishmael was the son of Nethaniah, a descendant of Elishama (One of the sons of King David) Ishmael led the killing of Gedeliah **(I Chronicles 25:25)**. ***Meaning*** God Will Hear (Ish-may-el) Male

ISHOD He was a son of Hammeloketh (His mother). His father is unknown as he is not mentioned in the Bible **(I Chronicles 7:18)** ***Meaning*** A Man of Majesty also Renown One (Ee-shod) Male

ISHUAI A son of Asher from the tribe of Asher his brothers were Isuah, Imnah and Beriah, his sister was Serah. His Grandfather was Jacob **(Genesis 46:17)** ***Meaning*** Strong One (Ish-u-eye) Male

ISRAEL God gave Jacob the new name of Israel **(Genesis 32:29)** ***Meaning*** One Who Has Been Strong (Iss-ray-el) Male/Female

ISSACHAR The ninth born of Jacobs twelve sons and founder of the Tribe of ISRAEL, ISSACHAR. He was the fifth born son of Jacobs first wife Leah. His brothers were Asher, Benjamin, Dan, Gad, Joseph, Judah, Levi, Naphtali, Reuben, Simeon and Zebulun. His sister was Dinah. Issachar had four sons they were named Job, Tola, Phuvah and Shimron **(Genesis 30:17-18)**. ***Meaning*** Recompense and He Will Bring a Reward. (Is-a-car) Male

ISUAH A son of Asher from the tribe of Asher his brothers were Ishuai, Imnah and Beriah his sister was Serah. His Grandfather was Jacob **(Genesis 46:17)** ***Meaning*** Strength (Ish-u-a) Male

ITHAMAR The fourth and youngest son of Aaron by Elisheba **(Exodus 6:23)** he was from a Priestly lineage **(I Chronicles 24:1-4)**. ***Meaning*** Coast of Palms (Ee-tha-mar) Male

ITHRA The father of Amasa **(2 Samuel 17:25)** ***Meaning*** Abundance (Eeth-raw)

ITHREAM A son of King David and Eglah **(2 Samuel 3:5)** ***Meaning*** Excellence and Profit (Eeth-ree-awm) Male

IZHAR He was one of the sons of Kohath, and grandson of Levi. His sons were Korah, Nepheg and Zichri **(Exodus 6:18,21) (Numbers 16:1)** ***Meaning*** Oil (Ee-Zar) Male

J

JAANAI A Gadite Chief **(1Ch 5:12)** ***Meaning*** Mourner (Jay-a-nye) Male

JAASIEL A son of Abner and a commander of the troops of Benjamin **(1 Chronicles 27:21)** ***Meaning*** Made of God and God is My Maker (Jay-ay-zee-ale) Male

JAALAM A son of Esau and Aholibamah **(Genesis 36:14)** ***Meaning*** Hidden (Jay-ay-lem) Male

JAAZANIAH A son of Shaphan. Ezekiel saw him in an act of idolatry **(Ezekiel 8:7,13)** Another Jaazaniah was a Jew from Maacha who joined forces with Gedaliah **(2 Kings 25:23)** and another was a son of Azzur **(Ezekiel 11:1,12)** ***Meaning*** Who The Lord Hears (Jay-az-a-nye-a) Male

JABAL A son of Lamech and Ada and a decendant of Cain. His brothers were Jubal and Tubalcain and his sister was Naamah who married King Solomon **(Genesis 4:20)** ***Meaning*** A Stream (Jay-bal) Male

JABIN A King of Hazor who rallied against Joshua with the Madon **(Joshua 11:1)** ***Meaning*** Wise One and He That Understands (Jay-bin) Male

JABESH Father of King Shallum of Israel **(2 Kings 15:10)** ***Meaning*** Dry (Jay-besh) Male

JACHAN A Chief Gadite in Bashan **(1 Chr. 5:13)**. ***Meaning*** Mourner or Troublesome (Jay-kan) Male

JACHIN see JARIB The fourth son of Simeon **(Genesis 46:10)** he was also called Jarib **(1 Chr. 4:24)**. Jachin was also the name of one of the two columns in Solomons Temple (The other was called Boaz) **(1 Kings 7:15,22)** ***Meaning*** He Will Establish (Jay-kin) Male

JACINTH or HYACINTH A precious stone with a pure orange color **(Exodus 28:19) (Revelations 21:20)**. ***Meaning*** Precious Gem (Jay-sinth) or (Hya-sinth) Female

JACOB The second born twin of Isaac and Rebekah and the Grandson of Abraham. His twin was Esau who sold his birthright to Jacob. Jacob always loved his cousin Rachel but was deceived by her father Laban (Rebekahs brother, his actual uncle) into marrying Labans other daughter Leah first, and forced to work for Laban for another seven years so he could later marry his beloved Rachel. Jacobs name was later changed to ISRAEL. Jacobs sons founded the twelve tribes of ISRAEL they were named Asher, Benjamin, Dan, Gad, Issachar, Joseph, Judah, Levi, Naphtali, Reuben, Simeon and Zebulun. These sons were born to four different women, Leah and her sister Rachel and Leahs servant (handmaid) Zilpah and Rachels servant (handmaid) Bilhah**(Genesis 25:29,34)**. ***Meaning*** Supplanter (Jay-cob) Male

JADA The son of Onam and brother of Shammai **(1Ch 2:28)** ***Meaning*** Knowing (Jay-da) Male

JADDUA Son of Jonathan and grandson of Joiada he was the last in the Levitical line from Eleazar mentioned in the Old Testament **(Nehemiah 12:11)** ***Meaning*** Known (Jay-do-a) Male

JAEL The wife of Heber, she was celebrated for a good deed in the song of Deborah and Barak **(Judges 4:17,22 and 5:24,27)** ***Meaning*** One That Ascends or A Kid (goat) (Jay-el) Female

JAHAZ A town in Transjordon captured by King Sihon **(Numbers 21:23)** ***Meaning*** Dispute (Jay-haz) Male/Female

JAHAZIEL One of Davids warriors **(1 Chron 12:5)** Another was a levite priest **(1 Chron 16:6)** another was a son of Zechariah **(2 Chron 20:14)** ***Meaning*** Seeing God (Ja-hay-zee-el) Male

JAHDAI A decendant of Caleb and the father of Jotham, Regem, Geshan, Pelet, Ephah and Shaaph **(1Ch 2:47)** ***Meaning*** To Grasp and To Hold

JAIR One was a judge of Israel **(Judges 10:3)**. And another was the Son of Segub and the grandson of Hezron **(I Chronicles 2:21-22)**. ***Meaning*** My Light (Jay-er) Male

JAIRUS One of the officials a Capernaum whose daughter was raised by Jesus **(Mark 5:21,43)** ***Meaning*** Who Difuses Lght and My Light (Jay-eye-rus) Male

JAKEH The father of Agur the author of some of the Proverbs found in the book of Proverbs **(Proverbs 30:1,14)** ***Meaning*** Pious (Jay-ka) Male

JALAM A son of Esau by his second wife Oholibamah **(Genesis 36:5)** ***Meaning*** Who God Hides (Jay-lam) Male

JAMBRES One of the two sages/magicians that confronted Moses and Aaron **(Exodus 7:11,22)** ***Meaning*** A Rebel (Jam-brez) Male

JAMES There are at least three James mentioned in the bible. The most prominent of these is James the disciple. He was the son of Zebedee and brother of John the disciple fisherman. The book of James is one of the first Catholic Epistles of the New Testament. Taken from the name Jacob ***Meaning*** He That Supplants or He That Undermines The Heel **(James 1:1)** (Jaym-ss) Male

JANNAI One of the ancestors of Jesus **(Luke 3:24)** ***Meaning*** To Answer (Jan-eye) Male

JANNES One of the two sages/magicians that confronted Moses and Aaron **(Exodus 7:11,22)** ***Meaning*** He Who Speaks Out or He Who Opposes (Jan-nez) Male

JANNEUS The Sir-name of Alexander Janneus the King of Judea. He was once a High Priest who was imprissoned. When he married Salome Alexandra (Which was not legal for a High Priest to do) he became King, his father was Aristobulus **(2 Mac 1:10 2:18)** ***Meaning*** Gateway or New Beginings (Jay-nee-us) Male/female

JAPHETH The last of Noahs three sons, brother to Ham and Shem and the father of seven sons named Javan, Magog, Madai, Tiras, Tubal, Meshech and Gomer **(Genesis 10:1)** ***Meaning*** May He Mulitply or May He Expand (Jay-feth) Male

JAPHLET or JAPHLETI One of the tribe of Asher and Grandson of Beriah, his sons were Ashvath, Bimhal and Pasach **(1Ch 7:33)** ***Meaning*** Delivered or Banished (Jaf-let) (Jaf-leti) Male

JAPHIA A son of King David by an unnamed wife **(II Samuel 5:13-16)** ***Meaning*** Enlightening and Appearing (Ja-fee-a) Male

JARAH A descendant of King Saul **(1Ch 9:42)** ***Meaning*** Honey Comb (Ja-ra) Male

JARED His father was Mahalalel and his son was Enoch (Enoch walked with God) he was the grandfather of Methuselah (Methuselah lived the longest 969 years) and he had many other children himself, he was a fourth decendant of Seth. He had a wife called Baraka (not mentioned in the KJV) **(Genesis 5:16-20)** ***Meaning*** Ruling and Commanding (Jar-red) Male

JARIB or JACHIN Jarib was one of the chiefs sent by Ezra to bring the Priests to Jerusalem **(Ezra 8:16)**. Another Jarib was a son of Simeon **(1Ch 4:24)** ***Meaning*** Avenging Fighting and Mulitplying (Ja-rib) Male

JARHA A servant of Sheshans, he was given his masters daughter Ahlai in marriage. They had a child named Attai **(I Chronicles 2:34-31)**. ***Meaning*** Servant or Humble (Jar-ha) Male

JASHAR From the book of the just. The Ancient book of Jashar or Yashar a Collection of ancient ryhme or song **(Joshua 10:12)** ***Meaning*** Of The Upright (Jay-sha) Male/Female

JASON The man that hosted Paul and Silas in Thessalonica **(Act 17:5-9)** he was related to Paul and accompanied him to Corinth **(Romans 16:21)** ***Meaning*** One That Cures (Jay-son) Male

JASPER The name of a gem that was found in the breastplates of High Priests **(Exodus 28:17,20)** ***Meaning*** Glittering (Jas-per) Male/Female

JAVAN He was one of the seven sons of Japheth. Javan had four sons himself named Elishah, Tarshish, Kittim and Dodanim **(Genesis 10:2)**. ***Meaning*** One Who Makes Sad (Jay-van) Male

JECAMIAH A son of King Jehoiachin (Jeconiah) of Judah **(1Ch 3:18)** ***Meaning*** Resurrection, Confirmation of The Lord (Jek-o-nye-a) Male

JECOLIAH She was the wife of King Amaziah of Judah **(2 Kings 15:2)** and the mother of King Azariah of Judah **(2Chron 26:3)** ***Meaning*** Perfection and Power of the Lord (Jek-o-lye-a) Female

JEDIDAH She was the wife of King Amon of Judah, mother of King Josiah of Judah **(II Kings 22:1)** ***Meaning*** Very Beloved (Jee-day-a) Female

JEDIDIAH A name given to Solomon by Nathan when he told David that Bathesheba had born him **(2 Sam 12:25)** ***Meaning*** Beloved of the Lord (Jed-ee-dye-a) Male

JEHIEL One of the sons of King Jehoshaphat of Judah who was killed by their brother, Jehoram (Joram) to try and consolidate his position as King **(II Chronicles 21:1)** ***Meaning*** Gods Living One (Jee-hye-el) Male

JEHOIACHIN or JECHONIAH A son of Jehoiakim one of the many Kings of Judah and father of Jecamiah **(1Ch 3:18) (Jer 24:1; 27:20)** ***Meaning*** Preparation and Strength of The Lord (Jee-hoy-a-kin) and (Jek-ko-nye-a) Male

JEHOADDAN Wife of King Jehoash (Joash) of Judah and mother of King Amaziah **(2 Kings 14:2)** ***Meaning*** Pleasure Time of The Lord (Jee-ho-a-dan) Female

JEHOAHAZ A King of Judah and the youngest son of King Jehoram **(2Ch 21:17; 22:1)** ***Meaning*** Possession of The Lord (Jee-ho-a-haz) Male

JEHOASH See JOASH A King of Israel, the son of King Ahaziah. His wife was named Jehoaddan. They had a son named King Amaziah **(2 Kings 14:2)** ***Meaning*** Fire of The Lord (Je-ho-ash) and (Jo-ash) Male

JEHOIADA The father of Beniah the leader of King Davids army **(2Samuel 8:18)** and father of Zechariah a Prophet of Judah **(2 Chron 24:20)** ***Meaning*** Knowledge of The Lord (Jee-hoy-a-da) Male

JEHOIAKIM or ELIAKIM A King of Judah and second son of King Josiah, his mother was Zebudah **(II Kings 23:36)**. He was the father of Jehoiachin and Zedekiah **(II Kings 24:6)** ***Meaning*** Whom God Will Raise Up (Je-hoy-a-kim) (Ee-lye-a-kim) Male

JEHONADAB A Nephew of King David by his brother Shemei **(2 Samuel 13:3)**. Another Jehonadab was the son of Rechab **(2 Kings 10:15)** ***Meaning*** Free Giver and Liberal One (Jee-ho-nay-dab) Male

JEHORAM or JORAM A King of Judah, the son of King Jehoshaphat and the father of Jehoshabeath and King Ahaziah **(I Kings 22:50) (I Chronicles 3:10-11) (II Kings 8:24)**. He was married to Athaliah, together they decreed all his brothers to be slain to strengthen his position as King **(II Chronicles 21:1-4) (II Kings 8:16-18, II Chronicles 21:6)**. His brother-in-law was also known as Joram/Jehoram and was also a King of Israel. ***Meaning*** Exaltation of The Lord (Jee-hor-ram) (Jor-ram) Male

JEHOSHABEATH or JEHOSHEBA She was the wife of Priest Jehoiada and the daughter of King Jehoram. She took Joash the son of her brother (King Ahaziah) and hid him so he would not be killed by her mother Athaliah, who decreed that all of the Kings sons be slain **(2Ch 22:11)**. ***Meaning*** Oath of The Lord and Fullness of The Lord (Jee-ho-sha-beth) (Jee-ho-she-ba) Female

JEHOSHAPHAT He was the son and successor of King Asa of Judah **(1 Kings 15:24)** and father of King Jehu of Israel ***Meaning*** The Lord is Judge (Jee-ho-sha-fat) Male

JEHOZABAD He was the son of Shomer. An officer in King Joashs army who rebelled and plotted against King Joash with Jozacars help, to bring the Kings downfall **(2 Kings12:21) (2 Chronicles 24:26)** ***Meaning*** The Lords Dowry (Jee-ho-za-bad) Male

JEHOZADAK or JOZADAK In the Levitical line of Eleazer, he was the son of Seraiah **(I Chronicles 6:14)** and the father of Jeshua **(Ezra 3:2)** ***Meaning*** Justice of The Lord (Jee-ho-za-dak) (Jo-za-dak) Male

JEHU Three Jehus in the bible. A prophet and son of Hanani **(2 Chron 20:34)**. Another was King of Israel (Successor to his father King Jehoshaphet). With Jehus help the prophecy of Elijah against Ahabs house came true **(1 Kings 15:24)**. Another Jehu was the son of Obed and father of Azariah **(I Chronicles 2:34-38)**. ***Meaning*** Who Does Exist (Jee-who) Male

JEHUDI A son of Nethaniah, Jehudi was a dignitary in the court of King Jehoiakim he read the oracles of Jeremiah to the King which predicted the end of Jehoiakims house **(Jeremiah 36:11,31)**. ***Meaning*** Praising God (Jee-who-dye) Male

JEIEL or JEHIEL There are six or more Jeiels in the bible. A brother of Beerah Prince of the Reubenites **(1 Chron 5:7)** and founder of Gibeon a benjamite **(1 Chron 9:35)**. Another was a Levite and chorister in the tabernacle **(1Ch 15:18,21)**. Another was a scribe during the reign of Uzziah **(2Ch 26:11)**. Another was a Levite who cleansed the temple **(2Ch 29:13)** A son of Adonikam, in exile who returned to Jerusalem with Ezra. Adonikam had 667 children **(Ezra 8:13)** ***Meaning*** Taken Away By God (Je-eye-el) ***Meaning*** Gods Living One (Jee-eye-el) Male

JEKAMIAH or JEKEMIAH A son of Shallum and father of Elishama (In the line of Sheshan through his daughter Ahlai) **(I Chronicles 2:34-41)**. ***Meaning*** Establishing or Revenging of The Lord (Jek-a-mye-ah) Male

JEMIMAH The first of three daughters of Job after his fortunes were restored to him. Jemimahs sisters were Keren (Keren-happuch) and Keziah **(Job 42:14)** ***Meaning*** Turtledove (Ja-mye-ma) Female

JEPHETH or JEPHTHAH A mighty man of valour who delivered Israel from the oppression of the Ammonites **(Judges 11:1-33)** ***Meaning*** Whom God Sets Free (Jay-feth) (Jay-fath) Male

JEPHUNNEH The father of Caleb and he was Joshuas companion exploring Canaan **(Numbers 13:6)**. Another was a Kenezite **(Joshua 14:14)**. Another was one of the descendants of Asher **(1Ch 7:38)**. ***Meaning*** He That Beholds (Jee-fun-eh) Male

JERAH One of the thirteen sons of Joktan, his brothers were Almodad, Sheleph, Hazarmaveth, Hadoram, Uzal, Diklah, Ebal, Abimael, Sheba, Ophir, Havilah and Jobab **(Genesis 10:25-30)**. ***Meaning*** Smelling So Sweet and also The Moon (Jee-rah) Male

JERAHMEEL The firstborn son of Hezron and father of Onam (Among many others) he had at least two wives including Atarah (The mother of Onam) **(I Chronicles 2:9, 2:25-27)**. A tribe in the desert of Palestine which later integrated with the tribe of Judah **(1 Sam 27:10))** ***Meaning*** The Mercy and Beloved of God (Jee-ra-mee-el) Male

JEREMIAH The second of the major Old Testament Prophets in the land of Benjamin, his father was Preist Hilkiah **(Jeremiah 1:1)**. Jeremiah dictated a scroll to Baruch who read the volume in the temple. Another Jeremiah was the father of Hamutal (His daughter) she was the wife of King Josiah of Judah **(2 Kings 23:31)** ***Meaning*** Exaltation of The Lord (Jer-ra-mye-ah) Male

JERIMOTH A son of King David by an unnamed wife, he was the father of Mahalath who became a wife of King Rehoboam **(II Chronicles 11:18)** ***Meaning*** Rejecter of Death (Jer-ra-moth) Male

JEROBOAM A King of Israel and father of King Nadab, he was the son of Nabat and Zeruah. **(1Kings 11:26)** Another was also a King of Israel and father of King Zechariahson, he was the son of King Jehoash ***Meaning*** He That Opposes The People (Jer-ro-bo-am) Male

JERUBBAAL or GIDEON Son of Joash **(Judges 6:11)**. Gideon had seventy sons to many wives **(Judges 8:30)** including Abimelech. After Gideons death Abimelech killed all but one of his half-brothers, he let Jotham live **(Joshua 9:5)**. He reigned for three years over Israel **(Joshua 9:22)**. ***Meaning*** Mighty Warrior (Jer-ru-ba-el) Male

JERUSHA A wife of King Uzziah of Israel and the daughter of Zaddok **(2 Kings 15:33)** ***Meaning*** Possession or Possessed (Je-ru-sha) Female

JESAIAH A son of Hananiah and grandson of Zerubabbel **(1 Chronicles 3:19, 21)** ***Meaning*** Salvation of The Lord (Jess-sye-ah) Male

JESHUR One of the three sons of Caleb, his brothers were Ardon and Shobab **(1 Chr. 2:18, 19)** ***Meaning*** Dear and Upright, Upstanding One (Je-shur) Male

JESHUA or JESHUAH A High Priest in the Levitical line of Eleazer who returned to Jerusalem from exile in Babylon **(Ezra 2:2, 5:2)** he was the son of Jehozadak **(Ezra 3:2)** and father of Joiakim and Jozabad **(Nehemiah 12:11) (Ezra 8:33)**. ***Meaning*** Savior and Deliverer of The People (*same as Joshua*) (Jesh-ua) Male

JESSE Grandson of Boaz and Ruth **(Ruth 4:17)**. Jesse was the son of Obed and father of King David. Jesse had eight sons and two daughters. Eliab was first, the second was Abinadab, the third Shimea, the fourth Nethanel, the fifth Raddai, the sixth Ozem and the seventh David. His daughters were Zeruiah and Abigail. Abigail was the mother of Amasa ***Meaning*** One Who is a Gift. Also means Stands Firm (Jess-ee) Male

JESUS or YESHUA or IESOUS The Son of God of whom the New Testament is written about, the one who came to live as an example for man ***Meaning*** Saviour and Deliverer (Jee-zuss) (Yes-shew-a) (Ee-sue-ss) Male

JETHRO A Priest and a Prince of Midian and the father of seven daughters including Zipporah who became a wife of Moses **(Exodus 2:16-21, 3:1)**. Moses tended the flocks of Jethro his father-in-law for forty years. Jethro was an Ethiopian and his father was named Reuel **(Acts 7:30)** ***Meaning*** Excellence or Excellent One

JETUR One of the twelve sons of Ishmael, his brothers were Nebaioth, Kedar, Adbeel, Mibsam, Mishma, Dumah, Massa, Hadad, Tema, Naphish and Kedemah **(I Chronicles 1:29-31)**. ***Meaning*** Order and Succession (Jet-tur) Male

JEUSH There are two Jeushs mentioned in the Bible. One was a son of Esau and Aholibamah **(Genesis 36:14)**. The other was a son of King Rehoboam and Abihail **(II Chronicles 11:18-19)**. ***Meaning*** He That is Devoured (Jeuz) (Jew-sh) or (Jew-z) Male

JEZEBEL The wife of King Ahab of Israel and the daughter of Ethbaal the King of the Zidonians **(I Kings 16: 30-31)** she fought against the prophets of the Lord and made her husband do evil things **(I Kings 21: 25)**. Jezebel was the mother of King Joram (Jehoram) of Israel **(II Kings 9:22)** ***Meaning*** Chaste One Female

JEZREEL His mother was Gomer and his father was Hosea the famous prophet. His brother was Lo-ammi and his sister was Lo-ruhamah **(Hosea 1:1)** ***Meaning*** God Scatters (Jez-ree-el) Male

JOAB Son of Zeruiah (King Davids sister) his brothers were Abishai and Asahel they were all great great grandsons of Boaz and Ruth **(1 Chron 2:16)** ***Meaning*** Patient and Helpful, Voluntary One (Jo-ab) Male

JOAH The third born son of Shimeath and Obededom. His brothers were Shemaiah, Sacar and Nethaneel **(1Ch 26:4)** ***Meaning*** A Fraternity or Brother of The Lord (Jo-a) Male

JOAKIM The Husband of Susanna **(Daniel 13:1)** ***Meaning*** Establishing of The Lord (Jo-a-kim) Male

JOANNA The wife of Herods steward who helped Jesus by giving of her possessions **(Luke 8:3)**. Joannna was one of the women who found Jesus tomb empty **(Luke 24:10)** ***Meaning*** Grace and Gift of The Lord (Jo-an-nah)

JOASH and JEHOASH The father of Gideon **(Judges 6:11)** A King of Israel, he was the son of King Ahaziah **(II Kings 11:1-2)**. When his father died his grandmother Ahaziah became queen and killed the lineage to the throne. Joash/Jehoash was hidden away by his aunt Jehosheba/Jehoshabeath and when Ahaziah was overthrown and killed he became King at the tender age of seven **(II Kings 20-21)**. ***Meaning*** Fire of The Lord (Je-ho-ash) (Jo-ash) Male

JOB Of the book of Job. A peaceful man from the land of Uz **(Genesis 46:13)**. Job was the son of Issachar founder of the tribe of Israel, Issachar. His grandfather was Jacob and his brothers were Shimron, Tola and Phuvah **(Genesis 30:17-18)**. ***Meaning*** He That Cries (Jo-b) Male

JOBAB One of the thirteen sons of Joktan his brothers were Almodad, Sheleph, Hazarmaveth, Jerah, Hadoram, Uzal, Diklah, Ebal, Abimael, Sheba, Ophir and Havilah **(Genesis 10:25-30)** ***Meaning*** Sorrowful (Jo-bab) Male

JOCHEBED She was the auntie of Amram, but she later married him and had children to him, these children were Moses, Aaron and Miriam **(Exodus 2:1 6:20) (Numbers 26:59)** ***Meaning*** Glorious and Honorable (Jok-e-bed) Female

JOEL The second of the Minor Prophets in the Old Testament. The namesake of the book of Joel. There are few Joels mentioned in the bible **(1Sa 8:2) (1Ch 4:35) (2Ch 29:12)(Act 2:16)** ***Meaning*** He That Wills or He That Commands and Jehovah is His God (Joe-ll) Male

JOHANAN In the Levitical line of Eleazer he was the son of Azariah and the father of another Azariah **(I Chronicles 6:9-10).** Another Johanan in the bible was the first son of King Josiah of Judah, he never became King himself **(1 Chron 3:15)**. ***Meaning*** One Who is Liberal and Merciful (Jo-han-nan) Male

JOHN John The Baptist son of Zechariah and Elizabeth a descendant of Aaron and cousin of Jesus **(Luke 1:5;36)** the gospel of John is his namesake. There is also another John, John the disciple a fisherman and the son of Zebedee, his brother was also a disciple named James. **(Matthew 10:2) (Mark 3:17) (Acts 1:13)** ***Meaning*** Grace and Mercy of The Lord (Joh-n) Male

JOIADA In the Levitical line of Eleazer, he was the son of Eliashib and father of Jonathan **(Nehemiah 12:10)** ***Meaning*** Whom Jehovah Favours (Joy-a-da) Male

JOIAKIM He was from the Levitical line of Eleazer. A High Priest and the son and successor to Jeshua (his father). He had a son named Eliashib **(Nehemiah 12:10)** ***Meaning*** To Whom Jehovah Has Set Up (Joy-a-kim) Male

JOKSHAN A son of Abraham by his concubine Ketura **(Genesis 25:1-2) (I Chronicles 1:32)**. He had two sons Sheba and Dedan. He had five brothers named Zimran, Medan, Midian, Ishbak and Shuah ***Meaning*** The Snarer The Hunter Catcher (Joke- shan) Male

JOKTAN He was one of the two sons of Eber. Joktan had thirteen sons named Almodad, Sheleph, Hazarmaveth, Jerah, Hadoram, Uzal, Diklah, Ebal, Abimael, Sheba, Ophir, Havilah and Jobab **(Genesis 10 25-30)** ***Meaning*** Little One or Little Contention (Joke-tan) Male

JONAH or JONAS Son of Amittai from the tribe of Zebulun **(2 Kings 14:25)**. Jonah is the namesake of the Book of Jonah and was swallowed by a great big fish, where he stayed in the belly of the fish for three days and three nights. Jonah is known as the reluctant prophet. ***Meaning*** A Dove (Jo-nah) (Jo-nass) Male

JONAM One of Jesus ancestors **(Luke 3:30)** ***Meaning*** A Gift From God (Jo-nam)

JONATHAN In the Levitical line of Eleazer, he was the son of Joiada and father of Jaddua **(Nehemiah 12:11)**. Also another Jonathan was the son of Careah/Kareah and brother of Johanan ***Meaning*** Given of God (Jon-na-than) Male

JORAM or JEHORAM A King of Judah, son of King Jehoshaphat and father of Jehoshabeath and King Ahaziah **(I Kings 22:50) (I Chronicles 3:10-11) (II Kings 8:24)**. He was married to Athaliah daughter of King Ahab of Israel **(II Kings 8:16-18, II Chronicles 21:6)**. His brother-in-law was also known as Joram/Jehoram A (King of Israel). Jehoram King of Judah killed all his brothers in order to strengthen his position **(II Chronicles 21:1-4)**. ***Meaning*** Exaltation of The Lord (Jee-hor-ram) (Jor-ram) Male

JORDAN The biggest river in Palestine, spoken of numerous times in the bible starting with Lot **(Genesis 13:10)** Meaning River of Judgement (Jor-dan) Male/Female

JOSEPH The eleventh born of Jacobs twelve sons, he was the first born son of Jacobs beloved second wife Rachel **(Genesis 30:22-24)**. Married to Asenath he was the founder of the Tribe of ISRAEL, JOSEPH. His brothers were Asher, Benjamin, Dan, Gad, Issachar, Judah, Levi, Naphtali, Reuben, Simeon and Zebulun. His sister was Dinah. He had sons named Manasseh and Ephraim, they each became founding fathers of their own tribes of Israel **(Joshua 16 & 17)**. ***Meaning*** Jehovah Has Added (Jo-sef) Male

JOSES One of the brothers of Jesus **(Mark 6:3,15:40)**. The name of Barnabas a Prophet and a good man, he was a friend of Pauls **(Acts 4:36)** ***Meaning*** Raised and One Who Pardons (Jo-sess) Male

JOSHUA or HOSHEA Namesake of the book of Joshua an Old Testament book about Canaan and the sharing of territory between the twelve tribes of Israel. Joshua is the son of Nun from the tribe of Ephraim **(Numbers 13:8)**. His birth name was Hoshea but was changed by Moses to Joshua and he was named as Moses successor **(Numbers 13:16)**. (Ho-say-ah) ***Meaning*** Salvation. ***Meaning*** Saviour and Deliverer of The People (Josh-ua) (same as Jeshua) Male

JOSIAH A King of Judah, he was the son of Amon. Josiah became King at the age of eight **(2 Kings 22:1)** ***Meaning*** The Fire of The Lord (Jo-zye-a) Male

JOTHAM The youngest son of Judge Gideon. He was the only one to survive the massacre of his brothers and half-brothers by his half-brother Abimelech (The son of Gideons concubine) **(Judges 8:30-31, 9:5)**. There are three Jothams in the bible. Another was the son of Azariah, King of Judah and ancestor of Jesus. **(2 Kings 15:5-7)** Yet another was a decendant of Caleb and the Son of Jahdai, whose brothers were Regem, Geshan, Pelet, Ephah and Shaaph **(1Ch 2:47)** ***Meaning*** Perfection of The Lord (Jo-tham) Male

JOZABAD From the Levitical line of Eleazer, he was the son of Jeshua and brother of Joiakim **(Ezra 8:33) (Nehemiah 12:10)** ***Meaning*** To WhomThe Lord Bestows (Jo-za-bad) Male

JOZACAR or JOZACHAR The second born son of Shimeath and Obededom. Together with Jehozabad son of Shomer, he rebelled and plotted against King Joash **(2 Kings12:21) (2 Chron 24:26) (1Ch 26:4)** his brothers were Shemaiah, Joah, Sacar and Nethaneel ***Meaning*** Jehovah Remembered or The Lord God Remembered (Jo-zak-car) Male

JOZADAK or JEHOZADAK In the Levitical line of Eleazer he was the son of Seraiah **(I Chronicles 6:14)** and the father of Jeshua **(Ezra 3:2).** ***Meaning*** Justice of The Lord (Jee-ho-za-dak) (Jo-za-dak) Male

JUBAL A son of Lamech by Adah and a decendant of Cain. His brothers were Jabal and Tubalcain and his sister was called Naamah **(Genesis 4:20)**. ***Meaning*** Music or Musical (Jew-bal) Male

JUDAH The fourth-born of Jacobs twelve sons and founder of the Tribe of ISRAEL, JUDAH. His mother was Leah **(Genesis 29:31-35)** his brothers were Asher, Benjamin, Dan, Gad, Issachar, Joseph, Levi, Naphtali, Reuben, Simeon and Zebulun. His sister was Dinah ***Meaning*** The Praise of The Lord (Jew-da) Male

JUDITH Daughter of Beeri the Hittite and wife of Esau **(Genesis 26:34)** ***Meaning*** Confession of The Lord and Praise (jew-dee-th) Female

JULIA A Christian woman who greeted Paul in Rome **(Romans 16:15)** ***Meaning*** Soft and Tender Hair (Jew-lee-a) Female

JULIUS A Roman centurion that had custody of Paul on the journey from Caesarea to Rome **(Acts 27:1,3)** ***Meaning*** Soft and Tender Hair (Jew-lee-us) Male

JUNIAS A Christain from Rome and a relative of Pauls he was sent to prison with Paul **(Romans 16:7)** ***Meaning*** Belonging to Juno The Principle Goddess of the Roman Pantheon (Jew-nee-ass) Male/Female

JUSHABHESED A son of Zerubabbel and grandson of Pedaiah **(1 Chronicles 3:19-20)** ***Meaning*** A Dwelling Place (Jush-sha-be-sed) Male

K

KADMIEL A Levite man **(Ezra 2:40)** ***Meaning*** Before The God of Antiquity and God of Rising (Kad-mee-el) Male

KAIN or CAIN One of the two sons of Adam and Eve. Brother of Able, whom he killed **(Genesis 4 :1)**. Cain was a tiller of the ground ***Meaning*** Fixed or Spear/Lance (Kay-n) Male

KAMON A city in Gilead **(Judges 10:5)** ***Meaning*** A Crest (Kay-mon) Male/Female

KANAH A town in Asher **(Joshua 19:28)** ***Meaning*** Of The Reeds (kay-nar) Male/Female

KAREAH or CAREAH Father of Johanan and Johnathon **(Jeremiah 40:8)** ***Meaning*** Ice (Kar-ree-ah) Male

KARNAIM A city found east of Galilee **(Genesis 14:5)** ***Meaning*** Horns (Kar-nay-im) Female/Male

KARTAH A town in the tribe of Zebulun **(Joshua 21:34)** ***Meaning*** Conversationalist and Social one (Kar-tar) Male/Female

KEDAR One of the twelve sons of Ishmael, his brothers were Nebaioth, Adbeel, Mibsam, Mishma, Dumah, Massa, Hadad, Tema, Jetur, Naphish and Kedemah **(Genesis 25 (I Chronicles 1:29)**. ***Meaning*** Dark Skinned (Key-dar) Male

KEDEMAH One of the twelve sons of Ishmael his brothers were Nebaioth, Kedar, Adbeel, Mibsam, Mishma, Dumah, Massa, Hadad, Tema, Jetur and Naphish **Genesis 25 (I Chronicles 1:29-31)**. ***Meaning*** From the East or Eastward and Ancient (Ked-ee-mar) Male

KEILAH A town in Judah **(Joshua 15:44)**. Also a descendant of Caleb **(1Ch 4:19)** ***Meaning*** A Citadel (Key-eye-lar) Male/Female

KELAIAH or KELITA A Levite man **(Ezra 10:23)** ***Meaning*** The Voice of The Lord and Gathering Together, Social One (Ke-lay-ya) Male

KEMUEL A son of Nahor **(Genesis 22:21)** ***Meaning*** Establish Him or Helper of God (Kem-you-el) Male

KENAN or CAINAN A son of Enosh/Enos and the grandson of Seth. One of Kenans sons was named Mahalalel who fathered Jared (who fathered Enoch in the lineage leading to Noah).

Kenan/Cainan married his sister Mualeleth (not mentioned in the KJV) **(Genesis 5:9,14)** Another Kenan/Cainan was the son of Arphaxad **(Luke 3:36)** ***Meaning*** Owner Possessor (Key-nan) (Kay-nan) Male

KEREN or KEREN-HAPPUCH One of the three daughters of Job born to him after his fortunes were restored. Her sisters were Jemimah and Keziah **(Job 42:14)** ***Meaning*** A Cosmetic Container (Key-ren) Female

KETURAH A concubine of Abrahams and the mother of six sons Zimran, Jokshan, Medan, Midian, Ishbak and Shuah **(I Chronicles 1:32)** ***Meaning*** Perfumed (Ket-toor-ah) Female

KEZIAH One of Jobs three daughters her sisters were Jemimah and Keren (Keren-happuch) **(Job 42:14)** ***Meaning*** Precious Perfume (Ke-zye-a) Female

KISH The father of King Saul **(1 Samuel 9:1)** ***Meaning*** A Bow (Kee-sh) Male

KISHI or KUSHAIAH The father of Ethan and a Levite who use to sing in the Temple during King Davids time **(1 Chron 15:17)** ***Meaning*** Hardness or The Lord Gravity (Kish-ee) (Koo-shay-ya)

KISHION A town in Issachar **(Joshua 19:20)** ***Meaning*** Hardness or Hard One (Kee-shy-on) Male/Female

KITTIM One of the four sons of Javan **(Genesis 10:4)** ***Meaning*** Gold Coloring (Kit-tim) Male/Female

KOHATH One of Levis sons **(Genesis 46:11)** and the father of Amram and grandfather of Moses, Aaron and Miriam **(Exodus 6:20)** ***Meaning*** Assembly (Ko-hath) Male

KORAH A son of Esau and Aholibamah **(Genesis 36:14).** Another Korah in the bible was the son of Izhar, his brothers were Nepheg and Zichri. His great grandfather was Levi **(Exodus 6:21)** ***Meaning*** Ice or Frost (Kor-ra) Male

KUSHAIAH see KISHI The father of Ethan a Levite who used to sing in the Temple during King Davids time **(1 Chron 15:17)** ***Meaning*** Hardness, The Lords Gravity (Koo-shay-ya)

L

LAADAH A son of Shelah **(1Ch 4:21)** ***Meaning*** To Assemble Together With Pleasure and Passing Over (Lay-ar-da) Male

LAADAN A descendant of Ephraim and father of Ammihud **(1Ch 7:26)** ***Meaning*** Pleasure (Lay-a-dan) Male

LABAN The brother of Rebekah **(Genesis 24:29)** A son of Bethuel **(Genesis 22:23)** He was the father of Jacobs wives, Rachel and Leah **(Genesis 29:16-28)** ***Meaning*** White (Lay-ban) Male

LADAN An ancestor of Joshua **(1Chron 7:26)** ***Meaning*** A Precious Metal or A Flower (Lay-dan) Male/Female

LAISH or LESHEM The father of Phalti **(1Sa 25:44)** and also a town near Jerusalem that was later named Dan after the tribe of Dan took it over **(Isaiah 10:30) (Joshua 19:47)** ***Meaning*** A Lion (Lay-ish) Male

LAISHAH A city of Benjamin **(Isaiah 10:30)** ***Meaning*** Good Strong and Courageous (Lay-ee-Shar) Female

LAMECH His father was Methuselah (Whom lived longest 969 years) a descendant of Seth (seventh in decent). Lamechs son was Noah. He had a wife called Betenos (not mentioned in the KJV) **(Gen 5:25-31) (1Ch 1:3)**. Another Lamech mentioned in the bible is the father of Jubal, Jabal, Tubalcain and daughter Naamah. He is a decendant of Cain, his father was Methusael **(Genesis 4:18-22)**. Lamech is the first person in the Bible to have two wives Adah and Zilah **(Genesis 4:19)** ***Meaning*** Made Low or Strikedown (La-mek) Male

LAODICEA A city in Asia Minor, Paul wrote a letter to the church in Laodicea **(Col 4:16) (Col 2:1)** ***Meaning*** A Just people or Just Person (Lay-o-de-see-a) Female

LASEA A town of Crete which Paul went through on his journey as a prisoner to Rome **(Acts 27:8)** ***Meaning*** Wise One (La-see-a) Male/Female

LASHA A city near the Dead Sea, southern end of Canaan **(Genesis 10:19)** ***Meaning*** Fissure or Dividing (Lay-sha) Female

LAZARUS The only man in all the parables to be given a name by Jesus **(Luke 16:19,31)**. Also Lazarus in the bible was Lazarus of Bethany, the brother of Martha and Mary who was resurrected by Jesus **(John 11)** ***Meaning*** Assistance of God and Who God Helps (Laz-zar-rus) Male

LEAH The daughter of Laban and sister of Rachel. Leah was given in marriage to Jacob deceitfully instead of Rachel (who Jacob truly loved). Jacob had served seven years working for Laban to secure Rachels hand in marriage. Laban gave him Leah on the wedding day instead. He was given Rachel as a wife a week later, but in return he had to serve Laban another seven years. Leahs auntie was Rebekah (Labans sister). Leahs children to Jacob were founders of the twelve tribes of Israel there names were Reuben, Simeon, Levi, Judah, Issachar, Zebulun and daughter Dinah. Leahs slave/handmaid Zilpah bore Jacob two children Asher and Gad. And Leahs sister Rachel bore Jacobs children Joseph and Benjamin. Rachels slave/handmaid Bilhah bore Jacobs sons Dan and Naphtali **(Genesis 29:15) (Genesis 29:32, 30:1)** ***Meaning*** Tired and Weary (Lee-ah) Female

LEBBAEUS The surname of the disciple Thaddaeus who was also called Judas or Jude. He was the son of James **(Luke 6:16) (Matthew 10:3)** ***Meaning*** Courageous (Le-bee-yus) Male

LEHABIM One of the seven sons of Mizraim his brothers were Casluhim, Ludim, Caphtorim, Naphtuhim, Pathrusim and Anamim **(Genesis 10:13)**. ***Meaning*** Flamed Swords (Lee-hay-bim) Male

LEHI The name of a town in Judah **(Judges 15:9,15)** ***Meaning*** Jawbone (Lee-hye) Male/Female

LEMUELThe name of a King of Massa who authored some Proverbs taught to him by his mother **(Pro 31:1,9)** ***Meaning*** Dedicated to God and God is With Him (Lee-moo-el) Male

LESHEM or LAISH The father of Phalti **(1Sa 25:44)** and also the name of a town near Jerusalem that was later named Dan after the tribe of Dan took it over **(Isaiah 10:30) (Joshua 19:47)** ***Meaning*** A Precious Stone (Lee-shem) Male

LEVI The third-born of Jacobs twelve sons, his mother was Leah. He was the founder of the tribe of Israel, LEVI **(Genesis 29:31-34)**. Because he and Simeon had killed Shechem (who had raped their sister Dinah and then arranged a marriage to her) **(Genesis 34)** they lost their birth-order rights to their brother Judah. Levis brothers were Asher, Benjamin, Dan, Gad, Issachar, Joseph, Judah, Naphtali, Reuben, Simeon and Zebulun. His sister was Dinah. Levis children were Gershon, Kohath, and Merari **(Genesis 49:1-12)** ***Meaning*** Associated With God or Friend of The Lords (Lee-vye) Male

LIBNI The First born son of Gershon and grandson of Levi, his brother was Shimei **(Exodus 6:17)** ***Meaning*** Whiteness (Lib-nee) Male

LILITH A demon or spirit who haunts the ruins in Canaanite folklore. Princess of the demons, also known as a night owl, she may have been called that because Lilith was originally the name of one of Adam and Eves daughters who became Adams second wife (Not in the KJV) **(Isaiah 34:14)** ***Meaning*** Night Monster (Lil-leth) female

LINUS A Christian man of Rome who sends greetings to Timothy **(2 Tim 4:21)** ***Meaning*** Net (lye-nuss) Male

LO-AMMI His mother was Gomer and his father was Hosea the famous prophet his brother was Jezreel and his sister was Lo- ruhamah **(Hosea 1:1)** ***Meaning*** Not my people (Low-arm-me) Male

LO-RUHAMAH Her mother was Gomer and her father was Hosea the famous Prophet. Her brothers were Jezreel and Lo-Ammi **(Hosea 1:1)** ***Meaning*** Not Obtaining Mercy (Low-Roo-Hay-Mar) Female

LOIS Mother of Eunice and the grandmother of Timothy who was praised by Paul for her sincere and endearing faith **(2 Timothy 1:5)** ***Meaning*** One Who is Better (Loy-ss) Female

LOT He was the son of Haran and had sisters called Iscah and Milcah. Abraham was Lots uncle. By devine intervention Lot and his family were to escape the destruction of Sodom and Gomorrah (A very wicked city) but Lots wife Ado (Her name is not mentioned in the KJV) turned to look back against Gods wishes and was turned into a pillar of salt. His two daughters got him drunk and had intercourse with him to protect their bloodline. They both had sons and the first was called Moab, he is the father of the Moabites unto this day. The other called her son Benami, he is the father of the children of Ammon unto this day **(Genesis 11:27)** ***Meaning*** Veil

LOTAN He was a son of Seir Duke of Edom, his siblings were Shobal, Zibeon, Anah, Dishon, Ezer, Dishan and his sister was named Timna. Lotans children were Hori and Hemam **(Genesis 36:20)** ***Meaning*** Coverer (Low-tan) Male

LUCAS/LUCIUS or LUKE The Author of the Third gospel the book of Luke and also The Acts of the Apostles **(Acts 1:1) (Luke1:1)** ***Meaning*** Luminous White (Loo-Kas) (Loo-See-Us) (Loo-K) Male

LUCIFER He was the Prince of the rebellious angels who fell from heaven ***Meaning*** Brilliant Morning Star (Loo-see-fer) Male

LUD One of the five sons of Shem and grandson of Noah, his brothers were Elam, Asshur, Arphaxahad and Aram **(Genesis 10:1,22) Meaning** Nativity Generation (Same as Ludim) (Loo-d) Male

LUDIM He was one of the seven sons of Mizraim. His brothers were Casluhim, Lehabim, Caphtorim, Naphtuhim, Pathrusim and Anamim **(Genesis 10:13)** ***Meaning*** Nativity Generation (same as Lud) (Loo-dim) Male

LUKE or LUCAS/LUCIUS The Author of the Third gospel the Book of Luke and of The Acts of the Apostles **(Acts 1:1) (Luke1:1)** ***Meaning*** Luminous White (Loo-Kas) (Loo-See-Us) (Loo-K) Male

LULUWA or AWAN The first daughter of Adam and Eve she married her brother Cain (not mentioned in the KJV) **(Genesis 39:12)** ***Meaning*** Beautiful One (Loo-Loo-wa) Female

LYCIA A city in Asia Minor that Paul visited **(Act 27:5)** ***Meaning*** A Wolf (Lie-See-a) Female/Male

LYDIA A woman who dealt with purple dye whom Paul converted to Christianity in Macedonia **(Acts 16:14)** Also an ancient city of Asia Minor ***Meaning*** Cultured Woman or Woman From Lydia (Lid-dee-a) Female

LYSIAS A Greek man whom assumed the name of Claudius after obtaining Roman Citizenship **(Acts 21:31-40)** ***Meaning*** Dissolving (Lye-see-ass) Male

M

MAACAH or MAACHAH There are four Maacahs in the bible. One was a daughter of King Talmai and the wife of King David. She was the mother of Davids children Absalom and Tamar **(2 Samuel 3:3)**. Another Maacah of the bible was one of the eighteen wives of King Rehoboam and mother of King Abijah. She was Rehoboams half cousin (By her fathers half-brother Absolom). Her father was Solomon **(I Kings 14:31) (II Chronicles 11:20-22)**. Another was the daughter of Abishalom and of Abijam (King of Judah) and grandmother to Asa. And another was one of Calebs concubines who bore him Sheber, Tirhanah, Shaaph and Sheva **(1 Chron 2:48)** **Meaning** Fastened or Secure One (May-ar-kah) Female

MAADIAH A Priest among the people who came back from Babylon **(Nehemiah12:5)** ***Meaning*** Pleaseant Testimony of The Lord (May-a-dye-a) Male

MAASAI A city in Judah **(Joshua 15:59*)*** ***Meaning*** Gods Work (May-a-see) Male/Female

MAASEIAH There are about six Maaseiahs in the bible the one of mention are, a son of King Ahaz of Judah **(2Ch 28:7)**. Another was the father of the priest Zephaniah **(Jeremiah 21:1 37:3)** Another was the father of the false prophet Zedekiah **(Jeremiah 29:21)** ***Meaning*** The Work of The Lord (May-a-see-ya) Male

MAATH One of the Ancestors of Jesus **(Luke 3:26)** ***Meaning*** Wiping Away and Absolving (may-ath) Male

MAAZIAH A priest who sealed the covenant with Nehemiah **(Nehemiah 10:8)** ***Meaning*** Strength and Consolation of The Lord (may-a-zye-a) Male

MACHAERUS A city east of the dead sea in Jordon (Not mentioned in the KJV) **(Mar 6:14-29)** ***Meaning*** Black Fortress (Ma-key-russ) Male/Female

MACHIR An ancient ancestoral tribe of Israel **(Judges 5:14)** A chief of the tribe of Manasseh **(1 Chron 7:16)** ***Meaning*** Selling (May-kir) Male/Female

MADAI One of the seven sons of Japheth, Madai was the third **(Genesis 10:2)** ***Meaning*** A Measure and Middle Land or Middle One (Mad-dye) Male

MADON A city of Canaan the people of Maydon rallied against Joshua with King Jabin ***Meaning*** A Chiding or Garment (May-don) Female/Male

MAGOG One of the seven sons of Japheth **(Genesis 10:2)** ***Meaning*** Covering (may-gog) Male

MAHALAH A son of Hammeloketh whose father is not mentioned in the Bible, the grandson of Manasseh **(1Ch 7:18)** ***Meaning*** A Dancer and a Harp (May-hal-la) Male

MAHALALEEL or MAHALELEL His great grandfather was Seth, his grandfather was Enos. His father was Cainan/Kenan. He had a son called Jared who fathered Enoch (the man who walked with God) Enoch fathered Methuselah, Mahalaleels great grandson. He had a wife called Dinah (not mentioned in the KJV) **(Genesis 5:12-17)** ***Meaning*** Praise of God (Ma-hal-la-leel) Male

MAHALATH or BASHEMATH There are two mentioned in the bible. One was a wife of Esau, her father was Ishmael and her brother was Nebajoth **(Genesis 28:9)**. Another was one of the eighteen wives of King Reheboam **(II Chronicles 11:18)** ***Meaning*** Lyre (May-ha-lath) Female

MAHALI A son of Merari, his brother was called Mushi from the line of Levi **(Exodus 6:19)** ***Meaning*** Infirmity or A Pardon (Ma-har-lee) Male

MAHARAI One of Davids warriors **(2 Samuel 23:28)** ***Meaning*** From a Hill (May-a-rye) Male

MAHLAH One of the five daughters of Zelophehad her sisters were Noah, Hoglah, Milcah and Tirzah **(Numbers 26:33)** ***Meaning*** Infirmity or Pardon (mar-la) (may-la) Female

MAHLI A Priestly family **(Exodus 6:19)** ***Meaning*** Weak (Mar-lee) Male

MAHLON A son of Naomi and Elimelech and the first husband of Ruth **(Ruth 1:2-4 4:10)** ***Meaning*** Weak (Mar-lon) Male

MAHSEIAH The grandfather of Baruch **(Jeremiah 32:12)**. Also his son was Neriah and his grandson was Seraiah (King Zedekiahs personal attendant) ***Meaning*** Anointed One (Mar-see-ya) Male

MALACHAI or MALACHI An Angel and messenger. The last of the Minor Prophets and writer of the last book of prophecies in the Old Testament **(Malachi 4:4,5,6)** ***Meaning*** Angel or Messenger (Mal-la-kye) (Mal-la-key) Male

MALCHIAH or MALCHIJAH There are three Malchiahs mentioned in the bible. A priest and the father of Pashur **(Jeremiah 21:1,11)**. Another was head of a division of priests **(1Ch 24:9)** Another was a son of Rechab who helped repair the gate of Jerusalem **(Nehemiah 3:14)** ***Meaning*** The Lord is My King (Mal-kee-ya) Male

MALCHIRAM Son of King Jehoiachin of Judah **(1Chron 3:18)** ***Meaning*** Of Exaltation (Mal-Key-ram) Male

MANAHEM A King of Israel **(2Kings 2 Kings 15:1)** ***Meaning*** The Consoler (Ma-na-hem) Male

MANASSEH The first of Josephs sons and the grandson of Jacob (Joseph and his eleven brothers founded the Twelve Tribes of Israel). His sons were Manasseh and Ephraim. Manasseh went on to found his own Israelite tribe MANASSEH, and his brother Ephraim founded the Israelite tribe EPHRAIM. Manasseh was a King of Judah **(Genesis 41:51)** ***Meaning*** God Has Made Me Forget (Ma-nass-eh) Male

MANOAH The Father of Samson from the tribe of DAN **(Judges 13:2)** ***Meaning*** Rest (Ma-no-ah) Male

MAOCH The Father of King Achish of the Philistine city of Gath **(1 Samuel 27:2)** ***Meaning*** Compressed (May-ok) Male

MAON A city of Judah **(Joshua 15:55)** ***Meaning*** House, Dwelling Place (May-on) Male/Female

MARCION A son of the bishop Sinope in Asia Minor **(Luke 6:43)** ***Meaning*** Shining and Gift (Mar-Shon) Male

MARCUS or MARK A disciple of Jesus **(Acts 12:12,25; 13:5,13)** ***Meaning*** Polite and Shining (Mar-k) Male

MARESHA Calebs first born son and the father of Hebron **(1Chron 2:24)** ***Meaning*** An Inheritance (Ma-ree-sha) Male

MARSENA A Prince of Persia **(Esther 1:14)** ***Meaning*** Of a Bramble (Mar-see-na) Male

MARTHA The sister of Mary and Lazarus **(Acts 17:19-21)** ***Meaning*** Bitterness (Mar-tha) Female

MARY There were three Marys of great note in the bible. One was the Mother of Jesus **(Luke 1;26)** Another was the sister of Martha and Lazarus **(Acts 17:19-21)** Another was Mary Magdalene from Magdala **(Luke 8:2)** ***Meaning*** Rebellion (Same as Miriam) (M-air-ree) Female

MASH or MESHECH One of the four sons of Aram **(Genesis 10:23)** ***Meaning*** Who is Force Drawn (Ma-sh) (Me-Shek) Male

MASSA One of the twelve sons of Ishmael, his brothers were Nebaioth, Kedar, Adbeel, Mibsam, Mishma, Dumah, Massa, Hadad, Tema, Jetur, Naphish and Kedemah **(I Chronicles 1:29-30)** ***Meaning*** A Lifting Up or A Gift of Prophecy (Mas-sa) Male

MATTAN Priest of Baal **(2Kings 11:18)** ***Meaning*** Gift of Rain (May-tan) Male

MATTANIAH see ZEDEKIAH Originally called Zedekiah a King of Judah **(2Ki 24:17)** ***Meaning*** A Gift of The Lord and Hope of The Lord (Mat-ten-nye-a) Male

MATTHEW He was also named LEVI and was a tax collector for the Romans. He became one of Jesus disciples **(Matthew 9:9,10; 10:3)** **(Mark 2:14)** ***Meaning*** Gift of God (Math-thew) Male

MATTATHA The son of Nathan and grandson of King David **(Luke 3:31)** ***Meaning*** His Gift (Mat-ta-tha) Male

MATTATHIAS An ancestor of Jesus **(Luke 3:25,26)** ***Meaning*** The Gift of The Lord (Mat-ta-thy-as) Male

MEDAN A son of Abraham by his concubine Ketura **(Genesis 25:1-2, I Chronicles 1:32)** ***Meaning*** Contention and Judgement (Mee-dan) Male

MEHUJAEL A son of Irad and descendant of Cain. He was the father of Methusael and grandfather of Lamech (Not the same person as Noahs father Lamech) **(Genesis 4:16-20)** ***Meaning*** One Who Proclaims God (Me-who-ja-eel) Male

MELCHI An Ancestor of Jesus **(Luke 3:24)** ***Meaning*** My King (Mel-kee) Male

MELCHIEL The Father of Charmis (The Magistrate) from Bethulia **(Judith6:15)** ***Meaning*** My King is God (Mel-Kee-el) Male

MELCHIOR He was one of the three wisemen. The other two were Caspar and Balthasar **(Matthew 2:1)** ***Meaning*** The Kings City (Mel-key-or) Male

MELCHIZADEK or MELCHIZEDEK A priest of Jesus **(Hebrews 5:6,10)** ***Meaning*** King of Righteousness and Justice (Mel-kez-za-dek) Male

MELEA The son of Menan and the father of Eliakim, one of Jesus ancestors **(Luke3:31)** ***Meaning*** Supplied and Full (Mee-lee-a) Male

MENAHEM A King of Israel **(2Kings 15:13,22)** ***Meaning*** The Comforter (Men-a-hem) Male

MENAN An ancestor of Jesus **(Luke 3:31)** ***Meaning*** Prepared and Rewarded (Mee-nan) Male

MERAB She was King Sauls daughter and the wife of Adriel, her sister was Michal and she had three brothers also **(1 Samuel 18:17)** ***Meaning*** Abundant One and also Fighting One (Meer-rab) Female

MERARI He was from the lineage of Levi and had sons named Mushi and Mahali **(Exodus 16:19)** ***Meaning*** Provoking and Bitter Sad (Mer-ra-ree) Male

MERIBAAL The Father of Micah **(2Samuel 9:12)** ***Meaning*** Man of Baal (Merri-ba-al) Male

MESHA A King of Moab **(2Kings 3:27)** ***Meaning*** Salvation (Mee-Sha) Male

MESHACH or MISHAEL The name given to Mishael, who was under training at the Babylonian court for the rank of Magi along with Shadrach and Abednego **(Daniel 1:7; 2:49; 3:12,30)** ***Meaning*** He That Draws With Force (Mee-shak) (Me-sha-el) Male

MESHECH One of the seven sons of Japheth and grandson of Noah his brothers were Gomer, Magog, Tiras, Javan, Tubal and Madai **(Genesis 10:2)** ***Meaning*** Who is Force Drawn (Mee-shek) Male

MESHULLAM A son of Zerubabble (The son of Pedaiah) **(1Ch 3:19)**. There are about eleven Meshullams in the bible. ***Meaning*** One Who Befriends (Me-shoo-lam) Male

MESHULEMETH Wife of King Manesseh of Judah and mother of King Amon **(II Kings 21:19)** ***Meaning*** Peaceful and Complete One (Mee-shoo-le-meth) Female

METHUSAEL A descendant of Cain, he was the son of Mehujael and the father of Lamech (different from Noahs father Lamech) **(Genesis 4:16-18).** ***Meaning*** A Man Who is of God (Meth-thew-say-el) Male

METHUSELAH He was the longest living man in the bible (969 years). His grandfather was Jared and his father was Enoch. Lamech was one of his sons, he was the Grandfather of Noah through his son Lamech (not the same as the Lamech as in Cains line fathered by Methusael). He was a descendant of Seth. He had a wife called Edna (not mentioned in the KJV) **(Genesis 5:21, 25-26)**. ***Meaning*** Man With a Dart (Meth-thew-sa-la) Male

MIBSAM One of the twelve sons of Ishmael, his brothers were Nebaioth, Kedar, Adbeel, Mibsam, Mishma, Dumah, Massa, Hadad, Tema, Jetur, Naphish and Kedemah **(I Chronicles 1:29)** ***Meaning*** Sweet Fragrance (Mib-sam) Male

MICAH The son of Meribaal and grandson of Jonathon and friend of King David **(2Samuel 9:12)** ***Meaning*** Humble Like The Lord (My-ka) Male

MICHAEL One of the sons of King Jehoshaphat of Judah who was killed by his brother Jehoram (Joram) as an attempt to consolidate his position as King **(II Chronicles 21:1-4)**. There are nine Michaels in the bible ***Meaning*** Who is Like God (My-Kal) Male

MICHAL A daughter of King Saul, she was given as a wife to David when he completed a challenge of bringing Saul the foreskins of 100 dead Philistines. David brought 200 foreskins **(I Samuel 18:17-27)**. But later Saul gave his daughter to another man named Palti **(I Samuel 25:44)**. She was eventually returned to David but Michal died childless **(II Samuel 3:14-16) (II Samuel 6:23)** ***Meaning*** Who is Perfect and Who as God (My-Kal) Female

MIDIAN A son of Abraham by his concubine Ketura **(Genesis 25:1-2) (I Chronicles 1:32)**. He had six sons Ephah, Epher, Hanoch, Abida and Eldaah. And he was the brother of Zimran, Jokshan, Medan, Ishbak and Shuah ***Meaning*** Covering Judgement (Mid-dee-an) Male

MILCAH There are two Milcahs in the bible. One was the daughter of Haran and sister of Iscah and Lot. She married her uncle Nahor and was the mother of eight sons including Huz, Buz and Bethuel **(Genesis 11:27, 22:20,22)**. Another is one of the five daughters of Zelophehad, her sisters were Mahlah, Noah, Hoglah and Tirzah **(Numbers 26:33)** ***Meaning*** Queen (Mil-kar) Female

MIRIAM Daughter of Amram and Jochebed and the sister of Moses and Aaron **(I Chronicles 6:3)** Miriam became a Prophet **(Exodus 15:20)** later she and Aaron opposed the marriage of Moses to an Ethopian woman **(Numbers 12:1)**. For this she was struck with leprosy **(Numbers 12:9-10)**. Aaron beseeched Moses, and Moses cried unto the Lord on her behalf, and she was healed **(Numbers 12:11-15)** ***Meaning*** Rebellion (Same as Mary) (Mir-ree-am) Female

MISHAEL or MESHACH One of Daniels friends, his name was changed to the Babylonian name Meshach **(Daniel 1:6;7)** ***Meaning*** Who is Like God (Mish-a-eel) Male

MISHMA There are two Mishmas mentioned in the bible. One was one of the twelve sons of Ishmael his brothers were Nebaioth, Kedar, Adbeel, Mibsam, Dumah, Massa, Hadad, Tema, Jetur, Naphish and Kedemah. **(I Chronicles 1:29-30)**. Also another was a decendant of Simeon **(1Ch 4:25,26)** ***Meaning*** Hearing (Mish-ma) Male

MIZRAIM One of the four sons of Ham and the Grandson of Noah, his brothers were Canaan, Cush and Phut **(Genesis 10:6)**. He was the father of seven sons Ludim, Anamim, Lehabim, Naphtuhim, Pathrusim, Caphtorim and Casluhim (out of whose line came the Philistines) **(Genesis 10:13-14).** ***Meaning*** Tribulations and A Fortress (Miz-ra-im) Male

MNASON A Christian from Jeruselem who received Paul into his home **(Acts 21:16)** ***Meaning*** Diligent Seeker (Nay-son) (*Silent M*) Male

MOAB The firstborn son of Lot and his daughter, she got her father drunk and had sexual intercourse with him in order to preserve his bloodline. Moab is the founding father of the Moabites **(Genesis 19:31-37)** ***Meaning*** Of His Father and Like His Father (Mow-ab) Male

MORDECAI The foster father of Esther **(Esther 2:7)** a Jewish captive in Persia **(Esther 2:5,6)** ***Meaning*** Contrition or Feeling Sorrow (Mor-dek-eye) Male

MOSES He was the very famous son of Amram and Jochebed, and the brother of Aaron and Miriam **(1 Chronicles 6:3)**. There were two wives recorded as being married to Moses, one was Zipporah by whom he had the sons named Eliezer and Gershom **(Exodus 18:2-4)** and the other was an Ethopian woman for whom no children are recorded **(Numbers 12:1)** ***Meaning*** Drawn Forth (Mow-zess) Male

MUALELETH She was the wife of Cainan/Kenan (he was her brother) (not mentioned in the KJV) ***Meaning*** Womanly (Moo-a-lay-lith) Female

MUSHI His father was Merari and his brother was Mahali from the line of Levi **(Exodus 6:19)** ***Meaning*** Receding or Takes Away (moo-shee) Male

N

NAAM One of the three sons of Caleb **(1Chron 4:15)** ***Meaning*** Pleasantness (Nay-am) Male

NAAMAH or NAHAMAH The daughter of Lamech and Zillah and a decendant of Cain. Her brothers were Jabal, Jubal and Tubalcaine. She married King Solomon (one of his 700 wives, but the only one named in the bible) she bore King Rehoboam to him **(Genesis 4:22)**. Also another very important Nahamah was Noahs wife (not mentioned in the KJV) ***Meaning*** Beautiful and Agreeable (Nay-a-ma) Female

NAARAI A warrior of King Davids, a military chief **(1Chron 11:37)** ***Meaning*** Youthful (Nay-a-rye) Male

NAASHON or NAASSON There are two Naashons in the bible. One was the brother of Elisheba (Aarons wife) **(Exodus 6:23)**. Another Naashon was one of Jesus decendants **(Matthew 1:4) (Luke 3:32)** ***Meaning*** He That Foretells (Nay-shon) (Nay-son) Male

NABAL A wealthy man who roused King Davids anger by not giving Davids men aid when asked. When David was later about to attack Nabal because of it, Abigail, Nabals wife persuaded David not to do so. Ten days after Abigails intervention Nabal died and shortly thereafter Abigail became Davids wife **(I Samuel 25:2-42)** ***Meaning*** Foolish (Nay-bal) Male

NACHON or NACON or NODAN or CHIDON The owner of a thrashing floor near which Uzzah was slain **(2 Samuel 6:6)** also called Chidon **(1Ch 13:9)** ***Meaning*** Prepared (Nay-kon) (Nor-dan) (Kee-don)

NADAB There are two Nadabs mentioned in the bible. On was a son of Shammai and the father of Appaim and Seled **(I Chronicles 2:28, 30).** Another was a son of Aaron by Elisheba **(Exodus 6:23)** he died without any children **(I Chronicles 24:1-2)** ***Meaning*** Liberal and Generous One (Nay-dab) Male

NAHALAL A town of Zebulun **(Joshua 19:15)** ***Meaning*** Pastures (Na-ha-lal) Female/Male

NAHALIEL A resting place on the way to Canaan **(Numbers 21:19)** ***Meaning*** Possession, Inheritance and Valley of God (Na-hay-lee-el) Female/Male

NAHASH King of the Ammonites **(2Samuel 10:2)** ***Meaning*** Serpent (Nay-hash) Male

NAHOR There are two Nahors mentioned in the bible. One was the father of Terah and Abraham as well as many other sons and daughters **(Genesis 11:22-26).** Another Nahor was the son of Terah and brother of Abraham and Haran, he married his neice (Harans daughter) Milcah **(Genesis 11:27-39).** Milcah bore him eight sons and with his concubine Reumah he had four sons **(Genesis 22:20-24)** ***Meaning*** Hoarse and Dry (Nay-hor) Male

NAHSHON The son of Amminadab. Nahshon was the father of Salmon **(Ruth 4:20)** ***Meaning*** Forteller (Nar-shon) Male

NAHUM The seventh minor prophet of the Old Testament and the namesake of the book of Nahum **(Nahum 1:1)** ***Meaning*** Comforter (Nay-hume) Male

NANAEA A Syrian Goddess **(1 Mac 6:2;2) (2 Mac 1:13,18)** ***Meaning*** Undefiled Straight and Virginal (Nar-nee-a) Female

NAOMI The wife of Elimelech and mother-in-law to Ruth and Orpah. When her sons Mahlon and Chilion and her husband were dead she told her daughters-in-law to return to their former homes **(Ruth 1:2-5)** Ruth stayed with her but Orpah left **(Ruth 1:10-18)** ***Meaning*** Lovable Delightful and Beautiful (Nay-oh-mee) Female

NAPHISH One of the twelve sons of Ishmael his brothers were Nebaioth, Kedar, Adbeel, Mibsam, Mishma, Dumah, Massa, Hadad, Tema, Jetur and Kedemah **(I Chronicles 1:29-31)** ***Meaning*** Refreshed Soul (Nay-fish) Male

NAPHTALI The sixth-born of Jacobs twelve sons and founder of the tribe of ISRAEL, NAPHTALI. He was the second son born to Bilah (Rachels handmaid). His brothers were, Asher, Benjamin, Dan, Gad, Issachar, Joseph, Judah, Levi, Reuben, Simeon and Zebulun. His sister was Dinah. **(Genesis 30:1-8)** ***Meaning*** He That Struggles or Wrestles and Fights (Naf-tar-lee) Male

NAPHTUHIM One of the seven sons of Mizraim. His brothers were named Casluhim, Ludim, Lehabim, Caphtorim, Pathrusim and Anamim. He is from Noahs lineage **(Genesis 10:13)**. ***Meaning*** To Open or To Carve (Naf-too-him) Male

NATHAN There are two Nathans mentioned in the bible. One was the son of Attai, grandson of Ahlai, (The daughter of Sheshan). He assisted David and he educated Solomon, he wrote about the life of David and of Solomon **(I Chronicles 2:34-36)**. The other mentioned Nathan was the son of King David by Bathsheba **(2Samuel 5:14)** ***Meaning*** Given and Giving (Nay-than) Male

NATHANAEL OR NATHANIEL A disciple of Jesus, also known as Bartholomew **(John 1:45-49, 21:2)** ***Meaning*** Given Gift of God (Nay-than-e-el) Male

NEBAIOTH see NABAJOTH The first-born of the twelve sons of Ishmael his brothers were, Kedar, Adbeel, Mibsam, Mishma, Dumah, Massa, Hadad, Tema, Jetur, Naphish and Kedemah. **(I Chronicles 1:29, Genesis 25:13)** his prophecies are found in the book of Isaiah **(Isaiah 60:7)** ***Meaning*** Prophecy or Prophetic One (Nee-bay-yoth) Male

NEBAT Father of King Jereboam of Israel **(1Kings 11:26; 12:2)** ***Meaning*** One That Beholds and Sees (Nee-bat) Male

NEBUCHADNEZZAR A King of Babylon who made his uncle Mathaniah (Zedekiah) a King, **(2 Kings 24:1)** Nebuchadnezzer was fond of deporting large populations and burning cities and temples ***Meaning*** Frontiers (Neb-u-kad-nez- zar) Male

NECO A Pharaoh of Egypt who was overpowered by Nedbuchadnezzar and lost rule of the western portion of Egypt to Babylonian Rule. His brother was named Eliakim **(2Kings 24:1)** ***Meaning*** Loyal One (Nee-ko) Male

NEDABIAH or NEDEBIAH A son of King Jehoiachin of Judah **(1 Chron 3:18)** ***Meaning*** Moved of The Lord (Ned-a-bye-a) Male

NEHEMIAH The cupbearer(A very trusted position) who helped rebuild his country, from the bible book of Nehemiah **(Nehemiah 1)** ***Meaning*** Comforted by the Lord (Nee-a-my-a) Male

NEHUSHTA She was the wife of King Eliakim of Judah and the daughter of Elnathan. She was the mother of King Jehoiachin **(2Kings 24:8)** ***Meaning*** Made of Brass or Copper (Nee-hoosh-ta) Female

NEPHEG There are two Nephegs mentioned in the bible. One was a son of King David by an unnamed wife **(2 Samuel 5:13-16).** Another was the son of Izhar, his brothers were Korah and Zichri. His great grandfather was Levi **(Exodus 6:21)** ***Meaning*** Weakened (Nee-feg) Male

NER The father of Abner (King Sauls Chief) **(1 Samuel 26:5)** ***Meaning*** Light (N-er) Male

NEREUS A Christian from Rome whom Paul greeted **(Romans 16:15)** ***Meaning*** Light and An Ancient God of The Sea (Ner-ree-us) Male

NERI An ancestor of Jesus **(Luke 3:27)** ***Meaning*** My Light (Nee-rye) Male

NERIAH The father of Seriah and Baruch (Jeremiahs scribe) **(Jeremiah 32:12)** ***Meaning*** Light of God and Lamp of God (Nee-rye-ah) Male

NERO The Emperor of Rome known as Nero Claudius Caesar **(Acts 25:1)** ***Meaning*** Powerful and Rebelious (Nee-row) Male

NETHANEL A brother of King David **(Numbers 1:8)** ***Meaning*** Given, Gift of God (Nee-than-el) Male

NETHANIAH There are two Nathaniahs mentioned in the bible. One was a descendant of Elishama and the son of King David, he was the father of Ishmael **(I Chronicles 25:25)**. Also another was the father of Jehudi **(Jeremiah 36:11)** ***Meaning*** Gift of The Lord (Nee-than-nye-a) Male

NETHANEEL The Fifth born son of Shimeath and Obededom. His brothers were Shemaiah, Jozacar, Joah and Sacar **(1Ch 26:4)** ***Meaning*** Given of God (Neth-than-nee-el) Male

NICANOR One of the seven deacons of the Apostolic Church **(Acts 6:1,6)** ***Meaning*** Conqueror and Victorious (Nee-ka-nor) Male

NICODEMUS A Jewish Rabbi and follower of Jesus whom meet with the Pharises to plead Jesus case (Not be condemned without a hearing). He also helped prepare Jesus body for burial **(John 7:45, 19:38)** ***Meaning*** Victory of The People (Nik-ko-dee-mus) Male

NICOLAUS He taught an unorthodox doctrine and could have been the resaon for Johns talk of Nicolaitans (Nik-ko-lay-ee-tanz) **(Revelations 2:6)** ***Meaning*** Peoples Victory or Victorious One (Nik-ko-lass) Male

NIMROD One of the six sons of Cush, he was a mighty man of the earth, a mighty hunter and warrior before the Lord, and ruler of the Kingdom. Nimrod was the one who led the people to build the Tower of Babel. He was from Ethiopia. His brothers were Seba, Havilah, Sabta, Raama and Sabtecha **(Genesis 10:7-14)**. ***Meaning*** Firm Rebellious One (Nim-rod) Male

NIMSHI He was the father of Jehoshaphat and the grandfather of King Jehu of Israel **(Kings 9:20)** ***Meaning*** Saved, Rescued (Nim-shy) Male

NOAH The famous son of Lamech (In the lineage of Seth). Noahs wife was Naamah/Nahamah and Noahs children were Shem, Ham and Japheth. Noahs story is about the flood. Noahs grandfather was Methuselah (The man who lived the longest 969 years) and his great grandfather was Enoch (The man who walked with God). When descendants of Cain and Seth began to inter-marry they became an ungodly and corrupted race. God entered into a covenant with Noah **(Genesis 6:7)**. Noah was told build an ark to save his family and some animals of the earth **(Genesis 6:14,16)**. The ark took 120 years to build **(Genesis 6:3)** and the world was then flooded with water and everything in it died. The ark floated for 150 days until finally settling on Mt Ararat **(Genesis 8:3,4)**. Noahs family then waited one year inside the ark before God gave them permission to leave it. Noahs mother was called Betenos (not mentioned in the KJV) **(Genesis 6-14)**. Another Noah mentioned in the bible was the daughter of Zelophehad **(Numbers 26:33** ***Meaning*** Rest (No-a) Male/Female

NOAM She was the wife of Enos (not mentioned in the KJV) ***Meaning*** Pleasantness or Pleasant One (No-am) Female

NOCHA or NOHAH A son of Benjamin **(1 Chron)** ***Meaning*** Rest and Calm (No-ka) (No-har) Male

NODAN also NACHON or NACON or CHIDON The owner of a thrashing floor near which Uzzah was slain **(2 Samuel 6:6)** also called Chidon or Nachon **(1Ch 13:9)** ***Meaning*** Aunt or Uncle (No-dan) Male

NOGATH or NOGAH A son of King David by an unnamed wife **(I Chronicles 3:7)** ***Meaning*** Brightness and Clearness (No-gath) (No-gar) Male

NOHAH or NOCHA A son of Benjamin **(1 Chron)** ***Meaning*** Rest Calm (No-har) (No-ka) Male

O

OBADIAH The master of the Palace in King Ahabs day **(1Kings 18:3)** ***Meaning*** Servant of God (O-ba-dye-a) Male

A-Z Of Hebrew Bibilical Names, Meanings, Bible References, Geneology and Pronunciations

OBAL One of the thirteen sons of Joktan **(Genesis 10:25-30)** ***Meaning*** Stripped (O-bal) Male

OBED There are two Obeds mentioned in the bible. One was a son of Boaz and Ruth and father of Jesse, Obed became the Grandfather of King David **(Ruth 4:17-22 Matthew 1:5 Luke 3:32)**. Another was the son of Ephlal and father of Jehu (in the line of Sheshan through his daughter Ahlai and his Egyptian servant Jarha **(I Chronicles 2:34-38)** ***Meaning*** Serving and Worshipping (O-bed) Male

OBEDEDOM The Husband of Shimeath and father of Shemaiah, Jozacar, Joah, Sacar and Nethaneel. His son Jozacar rebelled and killed King Joash **(1Ch 26:4)** ***Meaning*** Servant of Edom (O-bed-ee-dom) Male

OCHRAN The father of Pagiel from the tribe of Asher **(Numbers 1:13,2:27)** ***Meaning*** Troubler or One Who Troubles To or Trys To (O-Kran) Male

OHEL A son of Zerubabble and grandson of Pedaiah and decendant of David **(1 Chronicles 3:19-20)** ***Meaning*** Tent or House (O-hill) Male

OHOLAH and OHOLIBAH Two sisters representented as Samaria and Jerusalem in the book of Ezekiel **(Ezekiel 23:1)** ***Meaning*** Her Tent or Shelter or Tabernacle (Oh-ho-la) My Tent or Shelter or Tabernacle in Her (Oh-ho-lee-ba) Female

OHOLIBAMAH One of the wives of Esau **(Genesis 36:2)** ***Meaning*** Tabernacle or Tent of the Most High, Shelter of the Most High (O-holy-bar-ma) Female

OMAR The name of a tribe of Edom **(Genesis 36:11).** Also a son of Eliphaz grandson of Esau **(Genesis 36:11,15)** ***Meaning*** Eloquent, Very Well Spoken (O-mar) Male

OMRI The name of a King of Israel **(1Kings 16:15)** ***Meaning*** Servant of The Lord (Om-rye) Male

ONAM There are two Onams mentioned in the bible. One was a son of Jerahmeel by his wife Atarah, he was the father of Shammai and Jada **(I Chronicles 2:26)**. Another was one of the sons of Joiada he married a strange woman and was chased away from Nehemiah **(Nehemiah 13:28)** ***Meaning*** Strong (O-nam) Male

ONAN He was the son of Judah who was killed for refusing to have babies for his dead brother **(Genesis 38:4,8,10)** ***Meaning*** Strong One (O-nan) Male

ONESIMUS A slave of Philemon who ran away to Rome to see Paul and become a Christian **(Col 4:9 Philemon 1:10)** ***Meaning*** Profitable and Useful One (Owe-nee-see-mus) Male

ONESIPHORUS A Christian who helped Paul during his time in prison **(2 Timothy 1:16)** ***Meaning*** One Who Brings Profit (Owe-nee-see-for-us)

OPHIR One of the thirteen sons of Joktan his brothers were Almodad, Sheleph, Hazarmaveth, Jerah, Hadoram, Uzal, Diklah, Ebal, Abimael, Sheba, Havilah and Jobab **(Genesis 10:25-30)** ***Meaning*** Fruitful Region of Gold (O-fer) Male

ORPAH A daughter-in-law of Naomi and Elimelech, Orpah was the wife of Chilion **(Ruth 1:3,4,5)** ***Meaning*** Fawn (Or-pa) Female

OZEM A son of Jesse and a brother of King Davids **1 Chron 2:15)** ***Meaning*** Strong Man (O-zem) Male

OZIEL An ancestor of Judith **(Judith 8:1)** ***Meaning*** God is My Strength (O-zee-el) Male

OZNI A man from the tribe of Gad **(Numbers 26:16)** ***Meaning*** My Harkening, My Hearing (Oz-nee) Male

P

PAARAI He was one of Davids Warriors **(2 Samuel 23:35)** ***Meaning*** Opening of The Lord (Pay-a-rye) Male

PADON One of the Nethinim (Temple Servants) **(Ezra 2:44 Nehemiah 7:47)** ***Meaning*** His Redemption (Pay-don) Male

PAGIEL The son of Ochran from the tribe of Asher, a prince of the tribe **(Numbers 1:13,2:27)** ***Meaning*** God Allots To Me (Pay-gee-el) Male

PALLU or PHALU The second son of Reuben **(Genesis 46:9)** ***Meaning*** Hidden and Separated (Pay-loo) (Fay-loo) Male

PALTI The Benjamite who Saul gave his daughter Michal to, even though she was promised to David. She was given to David soon after though **(1 Samuel 25:43)** ***Meaning*** Deliverence (Pal-tye) Male

PALTIEL A son of Azzan from the tribe of Issachar **(Numbers 34:26)** ***Meaning*** Deliverance of God (Pal-tee-el) Male

PARSHANDATHA A son of Haman his brothers were Aspatha and Dalphon **(Esther 9:7)** ***Meaning*** Interpreter of Law and Given by Prayer (Par-shan-da-tha) Male

PASACH One of the sons of Japhlet from the tribe of Asher, his brothers were Ashvath and Bimhal **(1Ch 7:33)** ***Meaning*** Broken Piece of Clearing (Pay-sak) Male

PASHUR There are two Pashurs mention in the bible. One was the son of Immer he was governor of the temple and he beat and imprissoned Jeremiah. He was also the father of Gedaliah who persecuted Jeremiah. **(Jeremiah 38:1) (Jeremiah 20:1)**. Another was the son of Malchiah, both he and his father were Priests from a very influential family ***Meaning*** Extended, Mulitplying, Whiteness and Release (Pash-er) Male

PATHRUSIM One of the seven sons of Mizraim. His brothers were Casluhim, Ludim, Lehabim, Caphtorim, Naphtuhim and Anamim **(Genesis 10:13-14)** ***Meaning*** Land of The South (Pa-thru-zim) Male

PAUL or SAUL Also called Saul from the Tribe of Benjamin **(Act 8:1; 9:1; 13:9) (Romans 11:1) (Philemon 3:5)**. The book of Acts is dedicated to Paul and his life, visions and teachings. Paul was a preacher and a very important Christian of biblical proportions, he endured a great many persecutions throughout the New Testament ***Meaning*** Small, Little One (Paw-l) Male

PEDAHEL He was one of the Princes and Chiefs of the Naphtali tribe. The son of Ammihud **(Numbers 34:28)** ***Meaning*** Redeemed of God (Ped-a-hell) Male

PEDAHZUR The father of Gamaliel and leader of the Manasseh tribe **(Numbers 1:10,20)** ***Meaning*** Rock of Redemption, Strong One (Ped-da-zur) Male

PEDAIAH There are three Pedaiahs mentioned in the bible. One was the father of Zebudah who was the wife of Josiah and mother of King Jehoiakim **(2Kings 23:36)**. Another was the father of Zerubbabel and Pelatiahs great-grandfather **(1Ch 3:17,19)**. Another was the father of Joel, ruler of the tribe of Manasseh **(1Ch 27:20)**. ***Meaning*** Redemption of The Lord (Ped-day-a) Male

PEKAH A King of Israel and the son of Remaliah who went to war with Ahaz King of Judah **(Isaiah 7:1)**. Pekah was a captain in the army of King Pekahiah of Israel until he killed him to become King himself **(2 Kings 15: 25-27)**. ***Meaning*** Open And At Liberty (Pee-ka) Male

PEKAHIAH A King of Israel and son of King Menahem. He reigned for two years before his Captain Pekah killed him (To become Kind himself) **(II Kings 15: 21,22,27)** ***Meaning*** The Lord Opens (Pek-a-hye-a) Male

PELATIAH A son of Hananiah and the grandson of Zerubabbel from the line of King David **(1 Chronicles 3:19, 21)** ***Meaning*** Deliverance of The Lord (Pel-a-tye-a) Male

PELEG One of the two sons of Eber he was the father of Reu and many others **(Genesis 10:25, 11:18)** ***Meaning*** Division (Pee-leg) Male

PELET A decendant of Caleb and the Son of Jahdai, whose brothers were Jotham, Regem, Geshan and Ephah **(1Ch 2:47)** ***Meaning*** Deliverance (Pell-lit) Male

PERESH A son of Machir and Maachah from the Manasseh tribe, his brother was named Sheresh **(1Chron 7:16)** ***Meaning*** A Good Horsemen (Per-resh)

PEREZ or PHAREZ One of the twins born to Judah and Tamar (The elder of the twins) his brother was called Zarah/Zerah **(Genesis 38:29)** from Pharez came the line of King David **(Ruth 4:18,22)** ***Meaning*** Division (Per-rez) (Far-rez) Male

PERSIA or PERSIS A Christian woman who met Paul in Rome **(Romans 16:12)** Also a very large empire from India to Ethiopia with 120 provinces **(Esther1:1)** ***Meaning*** Divides and Also A Horsemen/Horsewoman (Per-sis) (Per-sha) Female

PETER or SIMON or CEPHAS The Disciple and the son of Jonah **(Matthew 16:16,17,18)** Simon-Peter had a brother called Andrew who brought him to Jesus **(John 1:40,42)** ***Meaning*** A Rock or Stone (Pee-tar) Male

PHALTI or PHALTIEL A son of Laish. He was married to King Sauls daughter Michal who had originally been promised to David but was denied **(I Samuel 25:44)**. Phalti eventually had to give her to David though **(2Samuel 3:15-16)** ***Meaning*** Deliverance of The Lord (fal-tee) (Fal-tee-el) Male

PHILIP One of the twelve disciples. The fourth disciple to be called, John, Andrew and Peter became disciples first **(Matthew 10:3) (Mark 3:18)** ***Meaning*** Lover of Horses (Fil-lip) Male

PHINEAS or PHINEHAS Son of Eleazar and grandson of Aaron **(Exdodus 6:25)** In ancient Egypt the ***Meaning*** was Negro. *In modern Egypt the* ***Meaning*** Mouth of Brass or Bold One (Fin-nee-ass) Male

PHUT or PUT One of the four sons of Ham and Grandson of Noah, his brothers were Canaan, Cush and Mizraim **(Genesis 10:6)** ***Meaning***To Place or To Lay (Foot) or (Poo-t) Male

PHUVAH His father was Issachar founder of the tribe of Israel Issachar, his grandfather was Jacob and his brothers were Job and Phuvah **(Genesis 30:17-18) (Gen 46:13)**.***Meaning*** Splendid (Poo-var) Male/Female

POTIPHERAH An Egyptian priest of On, he was the father of Josephs wife, Asenath **(Genesis 41:45)** ***Meaning*** Scatters (Pot-tee-fee-ra) Male

R

RAAMAH He was one of the six sons of Cush and the father of Sheba and Dedan whose descendants are from Ethiopia. His brothers were Seba, Havilah, Sabta, Sabtecha and Nimrod (The mighty one) **(Genesis 10:7)** ***Meaning*** Greatness and Thunder (Ray-a-ma) Male

RACHELThe daughter of Laban. Rachel and her sister Leah were the wives of Jacob. Jacob worked seven years for Laban in the hopes he would marry his true love Rachel. After the marriage ceremony he found out he had been tricked into marrying Leah (Rachels sister) instead. He was given Rachel in marriage laster as well but had to work another seven years for Laban as payoff. After many years of barenness Rachel finally gave birth to Joseph and then Benjamin (Whom she died giving birth to). Benjamin and Joseph were the 11th and 12th sons of Jacob the 11th and 12th Tribes of Israel. Jacob had four sons by Rachels handmaiden Bilah, who she offered to her husband. Jacobs other sons came from Leah and Leahs handmaiden. **(Genesis 29,31:50)** ***Meaning*** Ewe, Sheep (Ray-ch-el) Female

RAKEM One of the grandsons of Maachah and Machir, his father was Peresh and his brother was Ulam **(1Ch 7:16)** ***Meaning*** Varigated and Multicolored (Raa-kem) Male

REBEKAH The wife of Isaac (her first cousin once removed). A daughter of Bethuel **(Genesis 22:23)** she was Labans sister **(Genesis 25:20) (Genesis 25:20)** ***Meaning*** A Noose (Ree-bek-ka) Female

RECHAB Father of Jehonadab **(2 Kings 10:15)** ***Meaning*** Chariot (Ree-Kab) Male

REGEM A decendant of Caleb and the Son of Jahdai, whose brothers were Jotham, Geshan, Pelet and Ephah **(1Ch 2:47)** ***Meaning*** Stoned and The Color Purple (Ree-jem) Male

REHABIAH The son of Eliezer and the grandson of Moses and Zipporah **(1Ch 23:17; 24:21)** ***Meaning*** Extent of The Lord (Ree-hab-bee-a) Male

REHOBOAM The Last King of the Unified Kingdom, son of King Solomon. Successor to Solomon as King **(1Kings 11:43) (2Ch 9:31)** ***Meaning*** Who Enlarges The People (Ree-ho-bow-em) Male

REMALIAH or REMELIAH Father of King Pekah of Israel **(2Kings 15:25)** ***Meaning*** Exaltation of The Lord (Rem-ma-lye-a) Male

REU A son of Peleg and father of Serug and other sons and daughters **(Genesis 11:18-21)** ***Meaning*** His Friend or His Shepard (Roo) Male

REUBEN The first born of Jacobs twelve sons and founder of the tribe of ISRAEL, REUBEN. His mother was Leah **(Genesis 29:31-32)**. Reuben slept with his fathers concubine Bilah, so Jacob took away his position as firstborn and gave it to his brother Judah **(Genesis 35:22)**. His brothers were Asher, Benjamin, Dan, Gad, Issachar, Joseph, Judah, Levi, Naphtali, Simeon and Zebulun. His sister was Dinah. **(Genesis 49:1-12)** ***Meaning*** Vision of A Son or Behold A Son (Rew-ben) Male

REUEL The father-in-law of Moses **(Exodus 2:18)** ***Meaning*** Shepherd of God or Friend of God (Rw-el) Male

REUMAH The concubine of Nahor (Abrahams brother) she had four children to him,Tebah, Gaham, Thahash and Maachah **(Genesis 22:20-24)** ***Meaning*** Lofty and Sublime (Rew-mar) Female

RIPHATH One of the three sons of Gomer **(Genesis 10:3)** ***Meaning*** Remedy (Re-fath) Male

RUTH The daughter-in-law of Naomi and Elimelech **(Ruth 1:2-4)** the wife of their son Mahlon **(Ruth 4:10)**. After Elimelech and his sons died **(Ruth 1:3-5)** Ruth accompanied her mother-in-law Naomi back to her country **(Ruth 1:11-18)**. She remarried Boaz (A rich man) whom she worked for **(Ruth 3:12, 4:13)** ***Meaning*** A Friend (Roo-th) Female

S

SABTECHA or SABTECHAH One of the six sons of Cush from Ethiopia his brothers were Seba, Havilah, Sabta, Raama and Nimrod (The mighty one) **(Genesis 10:7)** ***Meaning*** That Surrounds Me (Sab-te-ka) Male

SABTAH or SABTA One of the six sons of Cush from Ethiopia his brothers were Seba, Havilah, Raama, Sabtecha and Nimrod (The mighty one) **(Genesis 10:7)** ***Meaning*** Rest and Aged (Sab-tar) Male

SACAR The fourth born son of Shimeath and Obededom. His brothers were Shemaiah, Jozacar, Joah, and Nethaneel **(1Ch 26:4)** ***Meaning*** A Price (Say-kar) Male

SALAH or SALA Son of Arphaxahad and father of Eber **(Genesis 10:24)** ***Meaning*** Mission Ending (Say-la) Male

SALATHIEL A son of King Jehoiachin of Judah **(I Chronicles 3:17)** ***Meaning*** Asked of God (Say-la-thee-el) Male

SALECAH A city in Bashan **(Deut 3:10)** ***Meaning*** Travel Devoted, Travel Lover (Sa-lek-ka) Male/Female

SALMA One of the sons of Caleb **(1Ch 2:51,54)** ***Meaning*** Perfection or Perfect One (Sal-mar) Male

SALMON The son of Naason and father of Boaz **(Ruth 4:20-21, I Chronicles)**. Rachab was his wife and the mother of Boaz **(Matthew 1:5)** ***Meaning*** A Hill (Sal-mon) Male

SALOME The wife of Zebedee and mother of James and John **(Matt 27:56)** she was related to Jesus mother Mary **(John 19:25)**. ***Meaning*** Perfect One (Sal-low-me) Female

SAMSON He was the son of Manoah a Judge and a decendant of the tribe of Dan. His life story is given in Judges **(Judges 13 ,16)** Samson lived in service unto God. He married a Philistine woman called Delilah **(Judges 14:1-5)**. It was an unblessed union and soon his wife was taken from him and given to his companion **(Judges 14:20)**. Samson was angered and burnt the Philistines corn, in return they killed Delilah and her father with fire. This caused him to tear down the pillars of the temple **(Judges 15,16,17)** ***Meaning*** Of The Sun and Unto The Lords Service (Sam-son) Male

SAMUELor SHEMUEL He had a miraculous birth, his life is detailed in the books of Samuel **(1Samuel 1:7,20)** Samuel anointed both Saul and then David to be King **(1Samuel 9,16)** ***Meaning*** Heard of God (Sam-mew-el) (Shem-mew-el) Male

SANBALLAT A Horonite who was against the welfare of the children of Israel after their return to Jerusalem from exile **(Nehemiah 2:10)**. His daughter married one of the sons of Joiada (Son of the high Priest Eliashib) **(Nehemiah 13:28)** ***Meaning*** Secret Enemy (San-bal-lat) Male

SARAH or SARAI Daughter of Terah and Abraham (**Genesis 11:24-2) (Genesis 20:1,12)** Late in life she had a child, Isaac **(Genesis 21:1,7)**. The King of Gerar, Abimelech, was attracted to Sarah. Abraham said that she was his sister (which was true as she was his half- sister) because he thought he would be killed if the King knew she was his wife. Abimelech took Sarah but did not touch her because God gave him a warning in a dream, so he returned her to Abraham along with many riches **(Genesis 20:1-18)** ***Meaning*** Princess (Sa-ra) My Lady My Princess (Sa-rye) Female

SAPPHIRA The wife of Ananais **(Acts 5:9,11)** ***Meaning*** That Relates and Beautiful (Saf-fear-ra) Female

SARSECHIM A Babylonian prince in the days of Nebuchadnezzar **(Jeremiah 39:3)** ***Meaning*** Master of Wardrobe (Sar-see-kim) Male

SAUL First annointed King of the unified Kingdom of Israel by Samuel **(1Samuel 9:1,2)** Another was Paul *(see Paul)* ***Meaning*** Demanded or Asked For (Saw-l) Male

SEBA One of the six sons of Cush from Ethiopia, his brothers were Havilah, Sabta, Raama, Sabtecha and Nimrod (The mighty one) **(Genesis 10:7)** ***Meaning*** **One Who Turns (See-ba) Male**

SEGUB A son of Hezron through a later marriage of Hezron to an unnamed daughter of Machir. Segub was the father of Jair **(I Chronicles 2:21-22)** ***Meaning*** Elevated One or Raised

SEIR The Duke of Edom and father of Lotan, Anah, Shobal, Dishan, Dishon, Zibeon, Ezer and Timna **(Genesis 36:20)** ***Meaning*** Rough Hairy Tempest (See-er) Male

SEMIRAMIS She was Nimrods wife (not mentioned in the KJV) ***Meaning*** Dwelling Place of Deity or Dwelling Place of The Gods (Sem-mira-miss) Female

SEPHATIAH One of the sons of King Jehoshaphat of Judah who was killed by their brother, Jehoram/Joram as an attempt to consolidate his position as King **(II Chronicles 21:1-4)** ***Meaning*** The Lord Judges (Sef-fa-tye-a) Male

SERAH A daughter of Asher from the tribe of Asher her brothers were Imnah, Isuah, Ishuai and Beriah. Her Grandfather was Jacob **(Genesis 46:17)** ***Meaning*** Princess of Abundance (See-ra) Female

SERAIAH A Chief Priest in the Levitical line of Eleazer, he was the son of Azariah and the father of Jehozadak **(I Chronicles 6:14)** he was killed by the King of Babylon **(II Kings 25:18-21)** ***Meaning*** Prince of Jehovah (Ser-ray-a) **Male**

SERUG A son of Reu and father of Nahor (Abrahams grandfather) **(Genesis 11:20-26)** ***Meaning*** Branch (See-rug) Male

SETH Third son of Eve and Adam **(Genesis 4:25)**. Seth was the father of Enos and other (unnamed in the bible) sons and daughters. He had a wife called Azura (Adam and Eves second daughter) (not mentioned in the KJV) **(Genesis 39:12) (Genesis 5:6-8)** ***Meaning*** Appointed One (Sey-th) Male

SHAAPH There are two Shaaphs in the bible. One was the Son of Jahdai, whose brothers were Jotham, Regem, Geshan, Pelet, and Ephah (He was a decendant of Calebs) **(1Ch 2:47)**. The other Shaaph mentioned in the bible was born to Caleb by his concubine Maachah, he had siblings named Sheber, Tirhanah and Sheva **(1Ch 2:49)** ***Meaning*** Division (Shay-aff) Male

SHADRACH The name given to Hananiah who went with Daniel to see the King **(Daniel 1:7)** ***Meaning*** Tender One (Sha-rak) Male

SHALLUM or SHALEM There are a few of Shallums in the bible. One was Josiahs third son who succeeded his father on the throne and reigned over Judah for three months **(2 Kings**

23:31). Another was the son of Sisamai and father of Jekamiah from the lineage of Sheshan through his daughter Ahlai and his Egyptian servant Jarha **(I Chronicles 2:34-41)**. Or In the Levitical line of Eleazer, he was the son of Zadok and the father of Hilkiah **(I Chronicles 6:12-13)** ***Meaning*** Perfect and Agreeable (Shay-lem) Male

SHAMARIAH A son of King Rehoboam by his wife, Abihail **(II Chronicles 11:18-19)** ***Meaning*** Throne (Shay-ma-rye-a) Male

SHAMMAI He was the son of Onam and the brother of Jada. He was the father of Nadab **(I Chronicles 2:28)** ***Meaning*** My Name or Desolute (Shay-my) Male

SHAMMAH One of the sons of Jesse, he was one of Davids brothers **(1 Samuel 16:9)** ***Meaning*** Desolution or Desert (Shay-ma) Male

SHAMMUA or SHIMEA A son of King David by Bathsheba **(II Samuel 12:11-18)** ***Meaning*** The Hearing of Prayer (Shay-mia) (Shay-mua) Male

SHAPHAN Father of Ahikam, Ahikam was the father of Gedeliah **(2Kings 22:12; 25:22)** ***Meaning*** Coney or Little Rabbit (Shay-fan) Male

SHAPHAT The father of the Prophet Elisha **(1Kings 19:16)** ***Meaning*** Judge (Shay-fat) male

SHAREZER Known as Negal-Sharezer he was an officer of Nebuchadnezzer **(Jeremiah 39:3)** ***Meaning*** Treasurer (Sha-ree-zar) Male

SHEBA One of the thirteen sons of Joktan, his brothers were Almodad, Sheleph, Hazarmaveth, Jerah, Hadoram, Uzal, Diklah, Ebal, Abimael, Ophir, Havilah and Jobab **(Genesis 10:25-30)**. Also another Sheba was a son of Raamah and Jokshan , he was the brother of Dedan and grandson of Cush **(Genesis 10:7, I Chronicles 1:9)**. He was the grandson of Abraham and Ketura **(Genesis 25:3, I Chronicles 1:32)** ***Meaning*** An Oath (Shee-ba) Male

SHEBER One Calebs sons by his concubine Maachah, his siblings were Tirhanah, Shaaph and Sheva **(1 Chron 2:48)** ***Meaning*** BreaKing Hope (Shee-ber) Male

SHEBUEL The son of Gershom and grandson of Moses and Zipporah **(1Ch 23:16 and 26:24)** ***Meaning*** Captive of God (Shee-bu-el) Male

SHECHEM A son of Hamor, he raped Dinah the daughter of Jacob saying that he wanted Dinah as his wife, a marriage was arranged provided that all the Hivite males became circumcized. Two of Jacobs sons, Simeon and Levi wanted to avenge their sisters rape and took advantage of the pain of the circumcized Hivites and went and killed them all. Jacob was not pleased with his sons and took away there birth order rights **(Genesis 34)** ***Meaning*** Shoulder (See-kem) Male

SHELAH Judahs third son **(Genesis 38:2,5)** Also the father of Laadah **(1 Chron 4:21)** and son of Arphaxad **(1Ch 1:18)** ***Meaning*** That Breaks or Unties (She-lar) Male

SHELEPH One of the thirteen sons of Joktan his brothers were Almodad, Hazarmaveth, Jerah, Hadoram, Uzal, Diklah, Ebal, Abimael, Sheba, Ophir, Havilah and Jobab **(Genesis 10:25-30)**. ***Meaning*** Who Draws Out (Shy-lef) Male

SHELOMITH The son of King Rehoboam and brother of King Abija of Judah **(II Chronicles 11:18-20)**. Also another was a daughter of Zerubabbel and grandson of Pedaiah **(I Chronicles 3:19)** ***Meaning*** Peacefulness (shy-low-mith) Male/Female

SHEM One of the three sons of Noah (In the lineage of Seth) Shems grandfather was Lamech and his great grandfather was Methuselah **(Genesis 5:32)**. Shem was the father of Elam, Asshur, Arphaxahad, Lud and Aram **(Genesis 10:22).** ***Meaning*** Renown or A Great (Sh-em) Male

SHEMAIAH The First born son of Shimeath and Obededom. His brothers were Jozacar, Joah, Sacar and Nethaneel. **(1Ch 26:4)** Another was the son of Adonikam brother of Eliphelet and Jeiel, his father had 667 children **(Ezra 8:13).** ***Meaning*** He That Hears and Obeys The Lord (Shy-may-ah) Male

SHEMUEL A Prince of the tribe of Issachar **(1Ch 7:2)** ***Meaning*** Appointed by God (She-moo-el) Male

SHEPHATIAH There are a few Shephatiahs in the bible. One was a descendant of Perez **(Nehemiah 11:4)** Another was a son of King David by Abital **(2Sa 3:4 and 1Ch 3:3)** Another was a ruler of the tribe of Simeon **(1Ch 27:16)** ***Meaning*** The Lord That Judges (Shef-fat-tye-a) Male

SHERESH One of the sons of Maachah, he had a named Peresh **(1Ch 7:16)** ***Meaning*** Root (She-resh) Male

SHESHAN A son of Ishi and the father of a Ahlai (His daughter) **(I Chronicles 2:31)** because he had no son he gave his daughter to his Egyptian servant Jarha to marry to continue his line **(I Chronicles 2:34-35)** ***Meaning*** Lilly Rose and Joy (She-Shan) Male

SHEVA One of Calebs sons by his concubine Maachah, his siblings were Sheber, Tirhanah, Shaaph and Sheva **(1 Chron 2:48)** ***Meaning*** Vanity Fame and Elevated One (She-Va) Male

SHIMEATH She was the wife of Obededom and the mother of Shemaiah, Jozacar, Joah, Sacar and Nethaneel. Her son Jozacar rebelled and killed King Joash **(1Ch 26:4)** ***Meaning*** He That Hears, Obeys and is Famous (She-mee-ath) Female/Male

SHILOH A city in the tribe of Ephraim **(Judges 21:19)** ***Meaning*** The Peaceful One Sent (Shy-low) Male

SHIMEI A son of Pedaiah **(I Chronicles 3:19)** and grandson of Jehoiachin (Jeconiah) **(I Chronicles 3:17-18)** King of Judah **(Esther 2:6)**. Also a son of Gershon, Shimeis brother was Libni **(1Ch 6:17)** ***Meaning*** Hears and Famous One (She-mee-eye) Male

SHIMRON His father was Issachar founder of the tribe of Israel, Issachar. His grandfather was Jacob and his brothers were Job, Tola and Phuvah **(Genesis 30:17-18) (Gen 46:13)**. ***Meaning*** Watchpost (Shim-ron) Male

SHOBAB A son of King David by Bathsheba **(II Samuel 12:11-18)**. And another was one of the three sons of Caleb his brothers were Ardon and Jeshur **(1 Chr. 2:18, 19)** ***Meaning*** Returned (Show-bab) Male

SHOBAL Another of the sons of Seir Duke of Edom his siblings were Dishan, Zibeon, Anah, Dishon, Ezer, Lotan and his sister Timna **(Genesis 36:20)** ***Meaning*** Path or Pilgrimage (Show-ball) Male

SHUAH A son of Abraham by his concubine Ketura. And the brother of Zimran, Jokshan, Medan, Midian, and Ishbak **(Genesis 25:1-2, I Chronicles 1:32)** ***Meaning*** A Pit or Ditch (Shew-wa) Male

SIDON The first born son of Canaan and a grandson of Noah **(Genesis 10:1, 15)** ***Meaning*** Fishing or Fisher (Sid-don) Male

SILAS or SILVANUS He and Judas were chosen by the church to go with Paul and Barnabas on their return to Antioch **(Acts 15:22)** ***Meaning*** Wood (S-eye-lass) Of the forest (Sil-van-nus) Male

SIMON or PETER or CEPHAS The Disciple and the son of Jonah **(Matthew 16:16,17,18)** Simon-Peter had a brother called Andrew who brought him to Jesus **(John 1:40,42)** ***Meaning*** He That Hears and Obeys (Sye-mon) Male

SIMEON The second born of Jacobs Twelve sons, he was the founder of the tribe of ISRAEL, SIMEON. His mother was Leah **(Genesis 29:31-33)**. Because he and Levi had killed Shechem, who had raped their sister Dinah and then arranged a marriage with her **(Genesis 34) both** Simeon and Levi lost their birth order rights to their younger brother Judah. His brothers were also founding members of the twelve tribes of Israel, they were Asher, Benjamin, Dan, Gad, Issachar, Joseph, Judah, Levi, Naphtali, Reuben and Zebulun. His sister was Dinah **(Genesis 49:1-12)** ***Meaning*** He That Hears (Sim-mee-on) Male

SISAMAI A son of Eleasah and father of Shallum (In the line of Sheshan through his daughter, Ahlai and his Egyptian servant, Jarha **(I Chronicles 2:34-40)** ***Meaning*** House or Dwelling (Sis-a-may) Male

SOLOMON He was the King of the Unified Kingdom. Solomon was King Davids second son by one of Davids wives named Bathsheba. Solomon had seven-hundred wives and three-hundred concubines **(2Sa 12:24 and 1Ki ngs1:13,17,21)** ***Meaning*** Peaceful One (Sol-low-mon) Male

STEPHANAS She was a Christian woman of Corinth **(1Cor 1:16)** ***Meaning*** Crowned (Stef-fan-nass) Female

STEPHEN He was one of the seven deacons, who became a preacher **(Acts 7:60)** ***Meaning*** Crown **(**Stee-fan) Male

SUSANNA She was the wife of Joakim **(Dan 13:1)** ***Meaning*** Lily Rose (Suz-zan-a) Female

T

TABITHA or DORCAS *(Greek)* She was restored to life by Peter **(Act 9:36,41)** ***Meaning*** Gazelle and Clear Sighted (Ta-bee-tha) Female

TAHAN A son of Ephraim **(Numbers 26:35)** ***Meaning*** Beseeching and Merciful One (Tay-harn) Male

TAHASH The third son of Nahor (The brother of Abraham) and his concubine Reumah **(Genesis 22:24)** ***Meaning*** Clean Skin (Tay-hash) Male

TALMAI He was the father of Maacha (The wife of King David and mother of Absolom) who was King of Geshur, Absalom fled after Talmai had put Amnon to death **(2Sa 3:3 and 13:37)** ***Meaning*** Furrow, That Suspends The Waters (Tal-my) Male

TAMAR There are three Tamars mentioned in the bible. One was the wife of Er (Judahs firstborn son) **(Genesis 38:6)**. When God killed Er **(Genesis 38:7)** the levite custom was followed and she married Onan. When Onan displeased God, he was killed also **(Genesis 38:8-10)**. Later Tamar had twin sons Pharez and Zarah by her father-in-law Judah **(Genesis 38:11-30)**. Also another Tamar was a beloved sister of Absalom **(II Samuel 13:1)**, she was raped by her half-brother, Amnon **(II Samuel 13:11-15)**. Absalom later arranged to have Amnon killed **(II Samuel 13:28-29)**. Also Absalom called one of his daughters Tamar **(II Samuel 14:27)**. ***Meaning*** A Palm Tree (Tay-mar) Female

TARSHISH One of the four sons of Javan **(Genesis 10:4)** ***Meaning*** Contemplation or Contemplative One (Tar-shish) Male

TEMA One of the twelve sons of Ishmael his brothers were Nebaioth, Kedar, Adbeel, Mibsam, Mishma, Dumah, Massa, Hadad, Tema, Jetur, Naphish, and Kedemah **(I Chronicles 1:29-30)** ***Meaning*** Admiration (Tee-ma) Male

TERAH A son of Nahor, he was the father of Haran and Abraham **(Genesis 11:24-27)**. He was also the father of Sara (Sarai) Abrahams wife **(Genesis 20:11-12)** ***Meaning*** Breathe and Wandering One (Ter-ra) Male

THOMAS also DIDYMUS One of the twelve disiciples **(Matthew 10:3 Mark 3:18 Luke 6:15)** ***Meaning*** Twin (Tom-mas) Male

TIMAEUS The father of Bartimaeus, who was cured by Jesus of blindness **(Mark 10:46)** ***Meaning*** Honour (Tim-may-us) Male

TIMNA/TIMNAH A child of Seir Duke of Edom whose brothers were Dishan, Shobal, Zibeon, Anah, Dishon, Lotan and Ezer **(Genesis 36:20)**. Another was the concubine of Esaus son Eliphaz and mother of Amelek **(Gen 36:12)** ***Meaning*** Portion (Tim-na) Female/Male

TIMOTHY or TIMOTHEUS A disciple of Jesus and Pauls companion. Namesake of the books of Timothy **(2Timothy 1:4)** ***Meaning*** Honouring God (Tim-mow-thee) (Tim-mow-thee-us) Male

TIRAS One of the seven sons of Japheth **(Genesis 10:2)** ***Meaning*** Determination of Form, Thought, Imagination and Desire (Tye-ras) Male

TIRHANAH He was one Calebs sons by his concubine Maachah, his siblings were Sheber, Tirhanah, Shaaph and Sheva **(1 Chron 2:48)** ***Meaning*** Recourse (Teer-harn-nah) Male

TIRZAH One of the five daughters of Zelophehad, her sisters were Mahlah, Noah, Hoglah and Milcah **(Numbers 26:33)** ***Meaning*** Benevolent and Pleasing (Tear-zar) Female

TITUS The Namesake of the book of Titus. Titus was with Paul and Barnabas at Antioch and Jerusalem **(Galatians 2:1,3) (Acts 15:2)** ***Meaning*** Honourable One (Tight-tus) Male

TOBIAH or TOBIJAH He was an enemy of the Jews in the days of Nehemiah **(Nehemiah 2:10,19)** ***Meaning*** Pleasing to Jehovah and The Lord is Good (Tow-bye-ya) Male

TOBIAS A good man known for his mercy and help in burying the dead, from the tribe of Naphtali and the book of Tobit (Not in the KJV) ***Meaning*** Goodness of The Lord (Tow-bye-ass) Male

TOGARMAH One of the three sons of Gomer **(Genesis 10:3)** ***Meaning*** Bone (Tow-gar-ma) Male

TOLA He was the son of Issachar (The founder of the tribe of Israel Issachar) his grandfather was Jacob and his brothers were Job and Phuvah **(Genesis 30:17-18) (Genesis 46:13)** ***Meaning*** A Scarlet Serpent or Worm (toy-la) Male

TUBAL One of the seven sons of Japheth **(Genesis 10:2)** ***Meaning*** The Earth, The World (Chew-bal) Male

TUBALCAIN A son of Lamech by Zillah and decendant of Cain. His brothers were Jubal and Jabal and his sister was Naamah **(Genesis 4:22)** ***Meaning*** Worldly Possessing or Possession (Chew-bal-kay-n) Male

U

ULAM A son of Sheresh and Nephew of Peresh **(1Ch 7:16)** ***Meaning*** The Court and Their Strength (Yoo-lam) Male

URIAH or URIJAH The first husband of Bathsheba. King David had him sent into battle on the frontline so that he would be killed so David could marry Bathsheba instead **(II Samuel 11:3-27)** ***Meaning*** The Lord is My Light (Yoo-rye-ya) Male

UZ There are two men called Uz mentioned in the bible. One was one of the four sons of Aram and the grandson of Shem **(Genesis 10:23)**. Another was the eldest son of Abrahams brother Nahor **(Genesis 22:21** *The Revised Version*) ***Meaning*** Fertile One (Uz) Male

UZAL One of the thirteen sons of Joktan, his brothers were Almodad, Sheleph, Hazarmaveth, Jerah, Hadoram, Diklah, Ebal, Abimael, Sheba, Ophir, Havilah and Jobab **(Genesis 10:25-30)** ***Meaning*** A Wanderer (Yoo-zal) Male

UZZIAH A King of Judah **(1Kings 14:21)** ***Meaning*** The Lord is My Strength (Yoo-Zye-a) Male

UZZIEL A grandson of Levi **(Exodus 6:18)** ***Meaning*** Strength of God (Yoo-zye-el) Male

V

VAIZATHA A son of Haman **(Esther 9:9)** ***Meaning*** Pure Self (Vye-zar-tha) Male

VASHNI The firstborn son of Samuel, his brother was and Abiah **(1Ch 6:28)** ***Meaning*** Changed (Vash-nee) Male

VASHTI Queen Vashti was the wife of King Ahasuerus of Persia **(Esther 1:11)** ***Meaning*** Beautiful (Vash-tee) Female

Y

YESHUA The Hebrew name for Jesus (Not mentioned in the KJV) ***Meaning*** He Will Save (Yes-shoo-a) Male

Z

ZABAD A son of Nathan and father of Ephlal (In the line of Sheshan through his daughter, Ahlai and his Egyptian servant, Jarha **(I Chronicles 2:34-36)** ***Meaning*** A Gift (Zay-bad) Male

ZABDIEL An overseer of the priests who lived in Jerusalem **(Nehemiah 11:14)** ***Meaning*** Gift of God (Zab-dee-el) Male

ZADOK In the Levitical line of Eleazer, he was the son of Ahitub and the father of Shallum **(I Chronicles 6:12)**. Another was the High Priest during King Davids reign **(2Sa 19:11 20:25) (1Ch 15:11)** ***Meaning*** Righteous One (Zay-dok) Male

ZARAH or ZERAH One of the twins born to Judah and Tamar (The younger of the twins) his brother was called Perez/Pharez **(Genesis 38:29)** from Pharez came the line of King David **(Ruth 4:18,22)** ***Meaning*** Sunrise (Zar-ra) (Zee-ra) Male

ZAHAM A son of King Rehoboam by his wife, Abihail **(II Chronicles 11:18-19)** ***Meaning*** Impure (Zay-ham) Male

ZEBEDEE The father of James and John. Zebedee was a fisherman and both James and John took the occupation of there father before becoming disciples **(Matthew 4:21,20:20) (Mark 1:20)** ***Meaning*** Abundant Portion or One of Abundance

ZEBULUN The tenth born of Jacobs twelve sons and founder of one of the tribes of ISRAEL, ZEBULUN. He was the sixth born son of Jacobs first wife Leah. His brothers were Asher, Benjamin, Dan, Gad, Issachar, Joseph, Judah, Levi, Naphtali, Reuben and Simeon. His sister was Dinah. **(Genesis 30:16-20)** ***Meaning*** Dwelling or Habitat (Zeb-yoo-lun) Male

ZECHARIAH or ZACHARIAH There are three Zechariahs mentioned in the bible. One was the son of King Jehoshaphat of Judah who was killed by his own brother Jehoram/Joram (Because Joram wanted to be King) **(II Chronicles 21:1-4)**. Another was the son of Jehoiada. Another was King of Israel and son of King Jereboam of Israel. And another was the father of Abijah, the wife of King Ahaz. ***Meaning*** Jehovah is Renown (Zak-kar-rye-a) Male

ZEDEKIAH or MATTANIAH A King of Judah who succeeded King Jehoiachin/Jechoniah **(II Chronicles 36:9-11)** he was the son of King Josiah **(I Chronicles 3:15) (Jeremiah 1:3)** ***Meaning*** Righteousness of Jehovah (Zed-da-kye-a) Male

ZELOPHEHAD He had five daughters Mahlah, Noah, Hoglah, Milcah and Tirzah **(Numbers 26:33)** ***Meaning*** The Shade (Zee-low-fee-had) Male

ZEPHANIAH One of the Minor Prophets and the namesake of the book of Zephaniah **(Zephaniah 1)** ***Meaning*** The Lord is My Secret and Jehovah has Concealed (Zef-fan-nye-a) Male

ZERUAH She was the wife of Nebat (He was the father of Jereboam, King of Israel) **(1Kings 11:26)** ***Meaning*** Wasp or Hornet (Zee-roo-a) Female

ZERUIAH She had three sons Abishai, Joab and Asahel. She was the daughter of Jesse and great granddaughter of Boaz and Ruth. Her brothers were Eliab, Abinadab, Shimea, Nethanel, Raddai, Ozem and King David, her sister was Abigail. **(Ruth 4:17)** ***Meaning*** Tribulation of The Lord (Zee-roo-eye-a) Female

ZERUBABBEL A son of Pedaiah **(I Chronicles 3:19)** and grandson of Jehoiachin/Jeconiah **(I Chronicles 3:17-18)** King of Judah **(Esther 2:6)** he was the father of Meshullam and Hananiah, Hashubah, Ohel, Berechiah, Hasadiah, Jushabhesed and daughter Shelomith **(1 Chronicles 3:19) (1 Chronicles 3:20)**. ***Meaning*** Seed of Babylon (Zee-roo-bab-bell) Male

ZIBEON Another of the sons of Seir Duke of Edom his siblings were Dishan, Shobal, Zibeon, Anah, Dishon, Lotan and his sister Timna **(Genesis 36:20)** ***Meaning*** Iniquity That Dwells (Zib-bee-on) Male

ZIBIAH Wife of King Ahaziah of Israel and the mother of King Joash **(2Kings 12:1) (2Ch 24:1)** ***Meaning*** The Lord Dwells (Zee-bye-a) Female

ZICHRI The son of Izhar, his brothers were Korah and Nepheg. His great grandfather was Levi **(Exodus 6:21)** ***Meaning*** Remembered and Illustrious One (Zee-kree) Male

ZILLAH One of the two wives of Lamech (The son of Methusael). The other wife was named Adah **(Genesis 4:19,22,23)** ***Meaning*** Shadow (Zee-la) Female

ZILPAH Leahs handmaid and the mother of Gad and Asher from the Tribes of Israel, Gad and Asher **(Genesis 30:9-13)** ***Meaning*** Trickle From The Mouth (Zil-par) Female

ZIMRAN A son of Abraham by his concubine Ketura and brother of Jokshan, Medan, Midian, Ishbak and Shuah **(Genesis 25:1-2) (I Chronicles 1:32)** ***Meaning*** Singer and Vines (Zim-ran) Male

ZIMRI One the of many Kings of Israel and a Chief of the tribe of Simeon **(Numbers 25:6,8,14)** ***Meaning*** Praise Worthy (Zim-rye) Male

ZINA A son of Shimei **(1Ch 23:10)** ***Meaning*** Shining (Zee-na) Male

ZIPPORAH The daughter of Jethro (Jethro/Reuel was a priest of Midian) **(Exodus 2:18-21)** **(Exodus 3:1)** she was the first wife of Moses **(Exodus 2:21)** ***Meaning*** Beauty and Beautiful Bird (Zip-por-ra) Female

ZIZA He was the bother of King Abijah of Israel. A prince of Simeon **(1Ch 4:37-43)** ***Meaning*** Splendour (Zee-za) Male

ZOHAR The father of Ephron **(Genesis 25:9-10)** ***Meaning*** Brightness (Zow-har) Male

ZULEIKA She was Potiphars wife **(Genesis 39:12)** ***Meaning*** Fair Haired (Zoo-Lee-Ka) Female

NOTES

NOTES

To Paul, Milan, Aalija and Asher
x

www.ingramcontent.com/pod-product-compliance
Ingram Content Group UK Ltd.
Pitfield, Milton Keynes, MK11 3LW, UK
UKHW051136260726
13967UKWH00010B/3083

9 781411 616189